Going Right

A Logical
Justification for
Pursuing Your Dreams

LOGAN GELBRICH

ISBN-13: 978-0-578-45308-8 (Paperback)

Library of Congress Control Number: 2019900967

Front cover image by Laura Duffy.
Book design by Anna Thompson.
Editing by Jacob Lewis.

Printed by HTS Publishing, Inc., in the United States of America.

First printing edition 2019.

HTS Publishing, Inc.
110 Lincoln Blvd.
Venice Beach, CA, 90291

www.holdthestandard.com

*"You see in this world, there is one awful thing,
and that is that everyone has his reasons.*

--JEAN RENOIR AS OCTAVE IN
"THE RULES OF THE GAME"

To my mom and dad, Deborah and Jerry.

Thank you.

This is for everyone with a choice.

LOGAN GELBRICH IS in pursuit. I've known him for a decade and he's been in this state of pursuit more continuously over time than anyone I've ever taught, coached, or collaborated with. Like Renoir's "everyone," Logan has his reasons, and they're most definitely of a higher order than the average reader. He'd probably even accept a peculiar sort of bet on that, if only just for the opportunity to persuade you of the efficacy of this pursuit he's consistently, continuously been on for over 25 years. The intentional, researched, practiced pursuit of growth oriented decision-making and meaningful contribution that Logan has termed "going right."

I first experienced Logan's distinctive pursuit in 2008. I was teaching courses in organizational behavior, group dynamics, and leadership theory and practice at the School of Leadership and Education Sciences at the University of San Diego. As a student athlete, Logan couldn't complete the undergraduate Minor in Leadership Studies because the baseball schedule conflicted with the capstone course for graduating seniors in the program. He had been told by several administrators that if he couldn't make the classes because of his schedule, he wouldn't receive the Minor. Most people would face the inevitability and adjust accordingly. Not Logan. His decision-making process and his commitment to the goals he had set out to achieve drove him to escalate his situation to the professor. That professor was me.

That was the first time I experienced Logan's state of pursuit. He walked into my academic office with deference but determination and after hearing from him, I could see that the system was set up against him. He wasn't facing institutional malice, just unthoughtful, unconsidered planning that inadvertently impeded student athletes from achieving their academic goals. His argument was logical, his plea was inspiring, and his commitment to the program up until then was stellar, but we had no existing option to accommodate situations like his. I appealed to my Dean, citing Logan's commitment, drive, and dedication and I designed an independent study course that would fit the baseball schedule and fulfill the Minor requirements.

That was just the first time I would experience Logan utilizing logic, inspiration, and commitment to build an objective justification for pursuing his dreams. According to the definition presented in this book, it was also the first time I saw him *going right*.

In Going Right, Logan describes the process of using these decision-making components he has methodically been constructing and stress-testing for himself, others, and high-performing organizations over decades. Throughout these years, his diligence in reading, blogging, studying human development, mindset function, and decision-making literature has surpassed graduate level study. The benefits of that breadth of interdisciplinary study enabled him to consider the most influential concepts and frameworks available in this field.

Along the way, Logan came to a key realization about the hard-won, positive results of practicing more intentional, higher ordered decision-making in his own personal growth. The cognitive development he experienced as a result of making difficult choices while he was *involuntarily* the subject of adverse circumstances like the leadership course, could also be achieved as a result of making difficult choices while he was *voluntarily* making himself the object of adverse circumstances. This adversity invited on purpose, enabled him to develop and to continue developing.

Along the way, Logan discovered that you don't have to wait for adversity in life to happen to you in order to grow. You can construct adverse situations, or invite healthy resistance for yourself so you increase opportunities to make difficult decisions better and grow faster. He soundly argues that inviting adversity and related concepts like negative feedback, deliberate practice, deep work, directed failure, and social costs provides the opportunity to increase your own joy, fulfillment, and satisfaction. In addition, he richly illustrates that this learning not only benefits the individual contributor, but also provides the opportunity to contribute to the larger social system as well.

Being close to Logan as he authored this book allowed me the proximity to see how the very exercise of writing this book required and realized all of these adverse experiences from Logan both involuntarily and voluntarily. This has been yet another observation of Logan in a state of pursuit. Acknowledging that he had not yet reached his own full potential. That fundamentally, we are all designed to evolve and grow. Stretching audaciously to accomplish something he had not previously attempted or achieved—writing a book—required courage, grit, failure, disappointment, and so much more. It provided the type of voluntary adversity that would enable Logan to willingly push his own development, while it exposed him to the involuntary adversities inherent in any large scale project. All at once, in one book project, he provoked his own growth and provided a model and framework for others to push their own development.

I was Logan's coach during his early writing process, bolstering and stress-testing his concept creation, and supporting his cognitive development. While preparing to write this foreword, I reviewed my handwritten notes from months and months of conversations. I discovered a quote from Logan during our first meeting about the book. It says, "I'm voluntarily taking on adversity."

This quote epitomizes the state of pursuit Logan continues in—the relentless pursuit of his own development, his highest expression, and his most beneficial contribution to his local community and to the larger society. Even and especially in this book.

It's a formidable author and courageous human who dares to practice the very thing he advocates, while opening the lived process of his advocacy and practice up to the scrutiny and inquiry of readers. But that is what Logan has done with this book. Some of the ways Logan committed to his own going right process didn't make the final manuscript cut and, at the risk of offending his equally formidable humility, there are a few I'd like to mention.

- He committed to ride his bike every Tuesday morning on the way to a dedicated block of writing time. This slowed down his pace of travel, forced an empty mental transition time, busied his body with repetitive movement, and brought awareness to his breath, all in order to orchestrate the conditions for more creative flow states

- He committed to welcome and solicit any feedback he could get on his process or the concept, and to resist defensiveness, rather paying close attention to how it could represent new paths of growth for him and ultimately a better product for you.

- He committed to talking about the concept of going right to all dinner guests, family and friends, podcast interviewers, airplane seatmates, in order to refine, iterate, and strengthen all of his thinking within the context of his community, and beyond.

- He committed to taking an detached perspective on his own feelings of repetitiveness, discouragement, exasperation, and unavoidable moments of doubt or weariness with the manuscript. Rather than waiting to write until he felt only positive feelings about the project, he repeatedly chose full immersion into the learning and the task. He did so counterintuitively, but trusting that doing so would likely produce the positive feelings he wanted to have about the project.

- He committed to defining and staying connected to his deeper sense of purpose throughout the process. Here's how I recorded Logan focusing and committing to deeper, personalized purpose in my notes from one of our sessions: "This is my answer to the ultimate questions of 'what's my purpose?' and 'what's my utility?' I have a sense of duty, I guess, to communicate this. To be complicit in contributing to the best version of the world. This mind shift is the most effective expression of our human potential. It's my purpose to provide this alternative mental model, to what's out there."

As you read this book, you'll identify Logan's presentation of the sources and definitions of flow, feedback, community, immersion, and purpose as key concepts and components of going right. You'll also recognize these components as he offers illustrations of historical events that mobilized around these themes, and examples of astounding people who describe similar building blocks they utilized to achieve the extraordinary success they did. As the foreword author though, someone who usually holds a unique quality of perspective on the book's author, I implore you to hold in mind at each turn of this book, the immense efforts at integrity taken on by Logan himself as the author. It's rare that the architect of a model and author of the book can themselves be considered an illustration comfortably situated among the astounding people who describe their process for attaining dream-level successes. Logan can hold the standard these exemplars have in common in his authentic dedication to intentional process, personal ownership of practice, and fierce perseverance in real-world action. In fact, my perspective from one of the floor seats on this court, affords me the ability to declare his capacity to continually raise that standard.

If you come to this book motivated to learn and curious about the decision-making mindset required to achieve peak expression of your human potential, consider one of Logan's most noteworthy statements, "motivation can mobilize us, but it rarely sustains us." This insight lays bare the need for a sustainable, actionable framework that justifies the difficult, logical, sometimes unconventional decision-making required to remain in a state of pursuit, regardless of the state of our motivation. This type of adaptive, conscious, developmental pursuit will result in higher quality, more intentional decision-making. When pursuing your dreams, this type of decision-making brings more probable success, increased fulfillment, enhanced joy, more options, layered contribution, freedom to determine direction, and the courage to pursue your loftiest goals. Even if you don't end up achieving a big dream, the ancillary skills you learn and the cognitive development you'll cultivate from going right increase your value as a contributor and dreamer exponentially. Going right is a passionate, rigorously examined call to transcend the socialized, subjective reasons for making "good" choices, and commit to a more objective practice of perspective-taking, welcoming adversity, and the actionable, developmental pursuit of a richer life.

Going right and in pursuit with you,

Cara

CARA T. MILLER, MDIV, PHD
SOLANA BEACH, CALIFORNIA
NOVEMBER 2018

CHAPTER 1

THIS IS HOW IT STARTS

"THIS IS HOW it starts," I said to myself, staring out at a sea of blue jerseys and hats. Timeout was called on the field. The momentum was shifting, ever so subtly. I looked back to my teammates in the dugout and mouthed, "Well, how 'bout *this*, boys?" It was the bottom of the 9th inning and our team, The University of San Diego Toreros, was down 5-0 to the University of Minnesota Golden Gophers in an elimination NCAA regional College World Series game. But we had two men on, and you could feel palpable jitters coming from the Gophers.

The University of Minnesota's coach, John Anderson, made the traditionally slow walk to the mound to talk to Dustin Brabender, his starting pitcher. Things were unraveling for the Golden Gophers live on ESPN. They needed just three outs to send us, the favorites, home and catapult themselves into the National Championship round.

Future New York Yankee, Justin Snyder, had led off the ninth inning for us with a double. And even though our prospects looked bleak, all thirty teammates toed the top step of the dugout to see, not *if*, but *how* we'd find a way to get out of this jam. Jordan Abruzzo, our catcher/designated hitter, then moved Justin to third on a single.

After several minutes of chatter on the mound, Coach Anderson signaled to the bullpen for the left-hander, Kyle Carr. The sellout crowd was on their feet, a rising sea of Torero blue. That year, 2007, The University of San Diego was ranked 4th in the nation with a clear path to the College World Series in Omaha, Nebraska. Our success came so fast we had to borrow our neighboring San Diego State's facilities to play host to that year's tournament. Our multimillion-dollar facility, Fowler Park, would be erected three years later off of the surge of the applause that now filled the stadium.

Like many performances at this level, most athletes are so focused on the task at hand that they never notice the crowd or their peripheral surroundings. As a team, we were having fun. We were in the zone. We were a manifestation of a group executing on their goals. To fulfill our desire to be our best selves. To attain our peak expression. Going right. Though many players in that dugout would go on to play professional baseball, this moment was a culmination of a life's work for many of us. Every ounce of commitment, practice, and resilience had been exhausted to make it from little league to high school to college. From backyards, schoolyards, parks, municipal ball fields and, ultimately, a good old-fashioned game of baseball under the San Diego twilight. Judging by the deafening sound, signs of support, and painted faces, we were living a culminating moment that couldn't have been so without the path we paved to get here.

Our rally continued. Shane Buschini singled home Snyder, making it 5-1. Their wheels were falling off, and we were attacking. The energy in the building was intense, and we were feeding off of it. We had played in plenty of big ballparks across the country, but this was different. More than three thousand fans were on their feet for us. Win or lose, the only thing to do was to allow our peak performance to manifest itself.

Josh Romanski, our left-handed center fielder, hit a ground ball to the right side and Minnesota made a throwing error enabling both Abruzzo and Buschini to score. The next hitter, Daniel Magness, recorded the first out of the inning with a grounder, moving the runners to second and third. 5-3, with one out in the bottom of the ninth, and I was up. I walked up to the plate in a dream state. This scenario had played out in my imagination hundreds, if not thousands, of times. I was the game-tying run. I went through my long, pre-at-bat routine. Part delay, part psych-out for the pitcher, and part psych-up for me, I dragged the process out.

I was hunting for an outside fastball. I'd been visualizing it before I started my walk to the batter's box. I envisioned success before the public service announcer could finish his announcement: "Now batting, number four, Logan... Gelbrich." I walked into this at-bat with a vision and a plan no different than a motivated CEO or an Army Ranger on assignment. I stepped into the box confident. I'm more nervous writing this than I was standing there in front of a boisterous stadium and on national TV trying to hit a little white ball at ninety miles an hour. I was grateful to have earned a chance to participate in a moment like this. I had done the work, put in the time, and prepared myself mentally. It was go time.

Standing in the box, I saw the pitcher and felt a pervasive sense of calm. The stadium sounds melted away. First, it was just him, then his arm, then the ball. I took the first pitch. Ball. I stepped out, cleared my head and started the process over. Ball. Two and 0.

I was a cocky player. It made me better and enabled me to handle these types of pressurized situations. It was fun. I stepped out of the box again "I'm getting my pitch here," I thought. Fastball! I put a swing on the ball that was twenty years in the making. Strike one. I was excited, like an emotional gambler and paid the price. Two and one.

Baseball, like life, is a game of countless adjustments. If your opponent makes a mistake, you have to capitalize. I stepped into the box the same way I had hundreds of thousands of times before. Fastball! I decided, in what felt like the most drawn-out moment, that I was going to swing at this pitch. I saw it so clearly that I remember having enough time to be grateful and surprised. The ball back spun off my bat to right center field and the moment felt like slipping from slow motion into warp speed as if my world took on the velocity of the swing of the bat. It was as if the volume punched up to level ten. I ran at an angle to first base assuming I had a double. The noise of the crowd came back just as fast as my vision stormed into hyperspeed. The ball left the yard before I touched first base and I raised my fist high in the air. The stadium turned into mayhem. I rounded second base to see my teammates emptying the dugout, jumping over the rail, hugging, and waiting to meet me at home plate. I could have cried, but I was too happy. I took my helmet off and put my head down into the mob.

I still have a photo of the moment, which appeared on the cover of the San Diego Union-Tribune. I remember that moment with incredible clarity. More importantly, I respect the totality of that moment because I'd prepared for it and there was a particular expectation of it occurring. I worked and studied for it in the context of a baseball player. I understood this moment as the perfect intersection of my life's peak challenge and my life's peak preparation, or *flow*. The universe made sense. It was *easy*. Time was nearly stopped, and the emotion was the most precious joy I could ever imagine experiencing.

→ → →

The moment above may seem rare. It may seem unique. But it's no different than an experience anyone can have if you live life to your full potential. Getting it is never easy—it takes discipline and hard work and a level of resilience—but the reward is a fulfilling life that is full of peak expression.

Most worthwhile pursuits are fraught with struggle. People spend their lives trying to avoid pain, including failure. Nonetheless, these are universally prevalent forces in our lives. And it's this notion—that we should prevent pain and avoid failure—that is affecting our decision making. It should never be about pain vs. no pain, it should be how we're identifying the most important pursuits. We're giving up what we want out of life at every turn. We're telling ourselves we're just being reasonable in doing so.

The goal of this book is to lay the groundwork for the most productive decision-making models that guide our lives. To provide an objective justification for pursuing your dreams. With the right decision-making process, I will argue you'll have the courage to make better decisions and live a more productive life. Against all the odds. This is going right.

To make a logical justification for the pursuit of your dreams based on clear, practical advantages to doing so will require clear analysis. I challenge you to poke, prod, and hold my argument to critical analysis. The coming chapters will propose that going right is tangibly more advantageous because it invokes commitment, deep work, resilience, flow, and skill transfer that is impossible to replicate or beat.

Louis C.K., the renowned comedian, has a tactfully tragic bit where he claims that "Everything's amazing and nobody's happy." He is making fun of our inability to recognize the opportunity around us technologically but, more interestingly, he is highlighting how we, as individuals, often find ourselves in victimized positions of not just under-performance, but under-contribution. There's a lack of fulfillment, joy, and happiness. Objectively speaking, there's also a lack in utility. Simply put, we're capable of more.

This book makes the case that if you're subscribing to this

most common decision-making model—which rationalizes the concession of your peak expression for a socially reinforced safe zone—you're proceeding with one hand tied behind your back. The mindset that dominates much of our decision making will continually guide you to be less happy, less successful, and less fulfilling choices. Faulty logic is pandemic.

Since I was seven, I was driven to play professional baseball. I requested to play for as many teams as I could as often as I could. Every announcement about my future was met with an adult encouraging me to be reasonable instead. Every family friend, teacher, and relative wanted to know my backup plan. "Architecture? You love to draw." "Engineering? You're good at math." "Business? You have such an aptitude for management." And those same people, once I became a professional baseball player, begged me to hang on as long as I could and to enjoy every minute instead. After I left baseball, when I told people I wanted to open a gym that was big on coaching quality and short on industry bullshit, they warned me: "I hope you know how many $150 membership you need to sell to keep something like that up and running." Now, with the gym thriving they reassure our success with praise: "That's what happens when you stick to your guns and live your passion."

If you are making decisions about what to do with your time, you're crossing your T's and dotting your I's in an effort to be logical. The strategy people take most often is to get a reasonable job in a reasonable town and start a reasonable family. This is the road map. But it's a faulty map We, as a society, agree on logic so flawed that we are systematically conceding our best selves, in every category of life, and calling it *reasonable*!

When we, as individuals, follow our dreams and strive to be the epitome of our best selves, that decision will shape and mold us into the incontestable creatures we can become. It gives meaning, fulfillment, and enables us to do the only job we've ever had as a species: evolve.

If you want something, you need to *be* it. True love, career fulfillment, and lifestyle mastery are long, hard, painful processes that take millions of decisions, over and over again, to manifest. We are not the receivers of our reality. We make our world.

To find your way to going right, you must accept and face uncertainty, failure, and pain. No one loves failure, but those who are unwilling to admit it are unwilling to succeed. Consider that there has never been a champion effort without pain. Pick any noteworthy effort in any discipline: painter, sports star, musician, politician, or academic. I'll bet their story is disgustingly infested with failure, uncertainty, and pain. To this day, there hasn't been a single master of their craft who has gotten to the peak without real, down to the marrow pain. If failure and pain are so critical, and so guaranteed, in pursuit of our most idealistic outcomes, at some point, we ought to reconsider if avoiding failure and suffering is the name of the game.

Everything you want, everything everyone has ever wanted, is characteristically defined, in part, as a painfully enjoyable pursuit. We pop pills to avoid pain in the same way that we are willing to work a mindless job. When you bob and weave, dodging, and fleeing the richest experiences life has to offer, you're systematically giving up all possibility of success.

I'm not speaking to you from the finish line, waving you forward to join me. There's no such thing. I struggle to live my best life every day, and, I can only hope you can enjoy the benefits I've experienced through the practice of going right. What we'll talk about in the coming chapters are all of the things I've studied, learned, and observed that make pursuing your peak expression, and all of the dreams that come with it, a strategic advantage over the alternative. Results come not with a focus on the results but with a dedication to the process.

I'm going to give you a concrete logical justification for following your dreams. The results you live with are always at the mercy of your own hand, The only reasonable choice is to pursue your peak expression, which includes mastery and joy. It's this pursuit that fosters the curiosity that turns into commitment. This decision making puts us in a position to develop a large body of work. When we're moving towards our dreams, we work in deliberate practice, which has the power to yield faster, better results. This pursuit is naturally more resilient to adversity and will help you build transferable skills. Also, following your dreams produce an opportunity to experience flow. We'll even see that this decision-making model is ripe for teams and organizations.

Each chapter will introduce you to a concept. These stories will come from notable individuals, from me and many of the people in my life, as well as others I admire. You'll hear all about my journey from boyhood dreamer to adulthood dreamer. We'll find out how practical it is that Dave Grohl of Nirvana and Foo Fighters fame rocks stadiums rather than selling mortgages. How unsanctioned backyard stick fighting led a man to the UFC and ultimately Hollywood and start-up business fame. How a barista is so good at making lattes he's been crowned a world champion and is immune to unemployment. How a poor immigrant be-

came a hat maker to the stars. All of these stories are only possible because of a choice. When you choose what is often the path
of most resistance, everything is possible.

Now, let's get down to it.

CHAPTER 2

GOING RIGHT

CRAMMED INTO THE middle seat of a Boeing 737—the knees on my 6'3", 220-pound frame tattooed to the metal housing of the fold-out table in front of me—I was too excited for the weekend to complain about my discomfort. It was 2005, and I was traveling with twenty-nine of my University of San Diego teammates, dressed head to toe in cheesy matching jumpsuits on our way to College Station, Texas for the Domino's Pizza Baseball Classic.

As a freshman, I paid the price of having to take the middle seat. I reluctantly traded aisle seat with a shorter upperclassman. To my right was a civilian, what we egotistically called non-athletes.

We got to talking and after explaining that we were a baseball team (NOT a volleyball team)—and a really good one at that!—he perked up. He loved baseball, played it as a kid, and followed it religiously as an adult. I have had versions of this conversation a million times in my life, from high school to college and into pro ball. I specifically remember this guy's disposition as he made sure I knew exactly how lucky I was. He missed those freewheeling days and griped about the "way things go."

"Enjoy it while it lasts," he said. "Working a desk job isn't what it's cracked up to be. Delay the inevitable."

His point was clear. At some point, he stopped doing what he really wanted to do and settled for whatever he was doing now. He wasn't living or expressing in the way he wanted to.

Let's call my seatmate John (since I never got his actual name). John hated his job. He worked at a software company. He had a distinctly difficult time explaining what he actually did, which in turn fueled his frustration contrasting our lives. It got me thinking that if he couldn't explain the purpose of his work, then maybe he didn't have much of a purpose after all. His tone became more somber by the minute.

"Never take this time for granted," he said. "It's the time of your life. Forget money and settling down and getting a real job. It's a trap, brother."

The irony that this man, who had mailed in his life, was suddenly coaching me to do the opposite was not lost on me. It has always surprised me how adults reach out to uncompromised youth and coach them, completely unsolicited, to avoid the mistakes they made. John was literally begging me to not become him. I didn't have the guts to ask him why he wouldn't take his own advice, but that is a question that has plagued me as long as I can remember, and it has led me here.

Experiences like this helped me begin to see a problem in society. It's a ubiquitous refrain for people to say that we should all follow our dreams. Yet most people aren't doing that. They're doing the thing they said they would never do. And they continue down the same path even as everyone continues to talk about the dream life. It baffles me.

This is a problem. This is *the* problem.

When a huge percentage of the population is knowingly choosing to undercut their own efficacy, it creates a systemic problem. It doesn't just negatively effect the individual lives, it erodes communities as well. It's a double-edged sword of failure.

This fundamental problem is rooted in misperception. And, confoundingly, it's all too preventable. John took the expected path with his life because he genuinely thought that it was the most logical choice. Remember his warning—delay the inevitable. In John's world, we're living a deterministic reality. According to him, my fate would be the same unavoidable purgatory he now lives when I quit playing. It didn't occur to him to suggest that I create the life I wanted because to him that isn't a logical choice.

We don't really know what his thought process was, or how his life unfolded up until that point, but I think we can all agree that what he was putting out into the world wasn't his best self. He all but admitted that to me on the plane. There was an unmistakable feeling that this man was stuck. It wouldn't have mattered if he earned a raise, went on a fabulous vacation, or bought a new car. He still would have felt the stagnation he claimed to be experiencing. Maybe his curiosity and pursuit of a productive life stopped with athletics and now he's wading in murky, stagnant waters.

When it comes to John, it feels like he's stuck because developmentally he *is*. Either he knew what he wanted and chose not to explore it, he suppressed the desire to unearth his potential, or he determined the benefits of his current lifestyle outweighed the cons. The problem with each of these situations is the logic he faced. I'm willing to bet that if he saw the reasoning for pursuing his peak expression that there would be zero chance that would have taken the same path. This is precisely what I am about to deliver to you: an objective justification for the utility of pursuing your peak expression.

→ → →

I want to make the most persuasive case possible to provide you with the right rationale for pursuing your dreams. To begin with, it will be helpful for us to be on the same page about a few assumptions. Without proper assumptions, I won't get very far in making an articulate and convincing argument. Any effective argument must be based on agreeable premises.

COMMITMENT

Simply put, commitment is the dedication to a cause or activity. It is a willingness to give time and energy to something, to give over oneself, over a long period, to a particular effort. Commitment results in large, sustained bodies of work and follows through with agreements. In contrast, those with a lack of commitment embody pursuits and relationships that are shorter in duration, demonstrate less integrity on agreements and accumulate fewer significant bodies of work. By that measure, it's safe to assume that commitment presents greater utilitarian value than a lack of commitment.

DEEP WORK/PRACTICE

Deep work is the ability to concentrate on a demanding task without distraction. Deep work stretches people's cognitive abilities by focusing on and mastering information in an effort toward true craftsmanship. Deep work and deliberate practice are not merely the antithesis of shallow work and practice. In these states, people can demonstrate an incredibly intense focus, over an extended period, with no interruption, all of which can enable accelerated learning. Depth equals intensity and a limitless approach. Deep work is inherently challenging and, as a result, can elicit positive adaptation.

RESILIENCE

Resilience is toughness. It is the capacity to recover from difficulties and adversity. What is it about resilience that is so appealing? Life is full of uncertainty and, in any pursuit, there is an endless stream of adversity. The question is how one behaves and responds in the face of those pressures. Those who show resilience can carry through, creating relevance and value. In a world of unwanted outcomes, those with greater resilience will invariably fare better.

FLOW

Flow is a modern psychology term that describes someone who is fully immersed and involved in an activity. The concept of flow stems from the work of Mihaly Csikszentmihalyi, a Hungarian-American psychologist who we'll meet in depth later. Flow is characterized by the complete absorption where a person is only focused on their immediate actions. A more colloquial term for it may be "in the zone." There is a significant amount of mounting research that supports the notion that flow states represent peak human performance, and that flow allows for the effortless execution of peak expression from writing to athletics.

TRANSFERABLE SKILLS

The last major assumption we'll make is that practicing the prior attributes can develop generally valuable, transferable skills. Building a broad skill set can be transferred from one specific practice to another unrelated one. This is the notion that if you learn resilience in a highly ranked marching band in high school that you could conceivably deploy this specifically developed resilience in a general manner in your first (non-marching band) job, for example. I'm not referring to how to rewire an electrical outlet, but how we approach and wrestle with any decision or problem. These skills are highly transferable across an infinite spectrum of specific applications. Imagine what avenues open when someone knows deep-rooted commitment. What kinds of pursuits would benefit from deeper, more meaningful attention to them? Would greater resilience be beneficial for a soldier and a struggling young artist? Is there a relationship, career, or craft that wouldn't benefit from flow states? These individually earned skills can be transferred and applied elsewhere with tremendous value.

→ → →

Now that we have set a basic understanding of the terminology for going right let's dive into exactly what it means to go right. This approach will primarily center around your decision-making and the methods you use to reach your peak expression.

Imagine every decision we make in life as a fork in the road where one direction represents self-actualization and the other self-destruction. Decisions made by going right move us toward self-respect and away from self-sacrifice. Once you've internalized going right, you can use it for any type of decision. Choosing how you spend your life has many facets including, relationships, career, and hobbies, each one containing a lifetime of decision making.

The trouble is we often rationalize taking the wrong direction when we come to these forks in the road. Our heart wants to accomplish great things in our lives, yet we rationally argue that taking the easy, safe route is the most logical. It's our critical thinking mind that wants to interject and tell us to do the smart thing. But it's our logical mind which should be telling us to take the harder choice. Too many times our mind overrides our desires, and we end up with the result that we don't really want. But that's the trick because while we rationalize the easy choice, it's actually the harder, more demanding direction which is logically more sound. What we really want and the logical choice are actually the same thing.

These are big ideas with arguably bigger implications. These are not decisions, nor is this idealized approach, that should be taken lightly. What we're talking about is contributing to your own happiness or, conversely, self-destruction. One direction is seemingly daunting and challenging. And the other appears easy and practical. Self-sacrifice will always be an option and easier than self-respect. There is a veil of safety in taking that easy path. As a result, seeking the highest expression of yourself will feel like the more vulnerable pursuit. And it's rife with failure and adversity. But it will also bring out the best you.

As humans, we are often compelled by the path of least resistance. In that way, striving for self-actualization feels like a road built on uncertainty. Our natural human tendency is to lean heavily on the perceived certainty. The stage is set for a lot of self-sacrifices because even though we can make a case that going right is better, there's no shortage of information telling us that it will be harder. But compromising idealism and justifying it by calling it realistic will never lead us to a happy existence.

There's something to this challenging element. It's never easy. Is that a coincidence? There's good news and bad news. The bad news is that a component of real challenge is part of the foundation of going right. The good news is that challenge provides a critical stimulus to advance lives. Stress and adversity are required for progress.

The theory I'm expounding in this book is one I've thought about for most of my life. Going right, after all, isn't about something you try on like a pair of shoes. This is software for life. I believe I had an early start to this kind of thinking, relative to my peers because at a young age I had clarity and purpose about how I'd like to attack my life. It wasn't merely that I had lofty goals. I began a realistic, actionable pursuit of my goal at an early age. There isn't a race to learn this lesson, though. In fact, in a world where we think results are everything, I'm asking you to have a mindset that says the *process* is everything. Going right is a chance to be better than yesterday; more utility, more value, more rich experiences, more complexity, and more *you*.

The problem of these divergent approaches to decision making has persisted throughout my life. And it is glaringly apparent in the conversation I had with John on the plane. And it's this problem that is at the heart of this book. I had one plan (a Plan A) when I was young, which was to become a Major League Baseball player. This would, I knew then, take nothing short of a lifetime of effort. Achieving this goal would mean continually evolving and improving at a pace higher than my peers. There would be no guarantee, assuming I even stuck to the plan, that it would work out. It's fair to say that throughout my life I'd need to continue to be open to adverse outcomes, continuously improve, and maintain a diligent practice. A change of heart at any stage could render the prior work meaningless. I could get hurt, or I could discover that my very best looked more like varsity letterman rather than a New York Yankee. Plan A was exciting. It was chock-full of rich learning experiences, provided meaning and direction, and would come with one hell of a life's story.

On the other hand, it was terribly risky. I would be met with resistance the entire way, from my friends, teachers, and even extended family. In the face of the most challenging experience, I'd have to listen to authority figures reminding me that I should be smart, have a backup plan, and have a readymade answer for the question, "What are you going to do if it doesn't work out?

Looking back, my father and I had a clear understanding of the work entailed to meet my lofty goals. All of the intrinsic motivation in the world still doesn't give you a crystal ball to look into the future. I knew that becoming a professional baseball player would be extremely difficult and that the only chance I had was to work unimaginably hard to get there.

I vividly remember, as a nine-year-old, roaming the National Baseball Hall of Fame in Cooperstown, New York with my father. This is where people who are obsessed with baseball go on vacation. "Logan, come here," my dad called out from across one fabled, trophy-laden room.

"This is the Triple Crown," he pointed as I eagerly arrived at the glass case. "It's the most prestigious award a hitter can win."

"Oh, that's cool!" I responded, pointing several slots down on the empty space under the winners' names. "That's is where my name is going to go!"

My father looked sternly at me. Not out of pity or scorn, but because he heard the seriousness in my voice. He wasn't listening to a kid making an endearing comment. This was the first moment that I knew my father and I were on the same page about my goals and the subsequent accountability I placed on myself.

"You know what that means, right?" he said.

With one word, I explained I was fully aware of what the next decade and a half, putting in remarkable hours of training and likely breaking my heart along the way, would look like while chasing an impossible goal. "Yes," I said.

The quest to play Major League Baseball, like other professional sports, can be an exercise in futility. The percentage of players who actually make it is staggering. The year I was selected first overall in the Del Rey American Little League draft, 1996, 2.5 million kids were playing little league in the U.S. With just eight hundred Major League Baseball players, the probability of transcending the ranks from Del Rey American Little League to the MLB is only 0.0296%. At those odds, it doesn't work to sorta-kinda want to pursue the craft. Following your curiosity into real commitment is just the first step in going right. When your Plan A is big enough, it doesn't pay to have a Plan B.

Will Smith—actor, producer, and rapper—knows all about chasing and executing upon Plan A. His success is evident and on full display but despite his humble upbringing, Smith was given a scholarship as an undergraduate to attend MIT. Against the wishes of his family, he declined the opportunity and moved to Los Angeles. Soon after his music and acting launched him into stardom. Life presented Smith with a remarkable "Plan B." In an interview on The Early Show on CBS, Smith talked about his commitment to Plan A. "The first step before anyone else in the world believes it, is you have to believe it," Smith said. "There's no reason to have a Plan B because it distracts from Plan A."

When we look at the career of a Will Smith, someone who's enjoying the highest levels of his career, we don't see someone who's having to make difficult choices. While on a press tour for his film, "The Pursuit of Happiness," Smith spoke about whether other people should be realistic their own decision making. "Being realistic," Smith said, "is the most commonly traveled road to mediocrity. Why would you be realistic? What's the point of being realistic? It's unrealistic to walk into a room and flip a switch and lights come on. That's unrealistic. Fortunately, Edison didn't think so. It's unrealistic to think you're going to bend a piece of metal and fly people over an ocean. That's unrealistic, but fortunately, the Wright brothers and others didn't believe that. It seems like such a ridiculous idea to me to embrace the idea that it's not going to happen and that's not real for that to happen. As soon as you say it, now you just made that real!"

This kind of decision making can be a catch-22. There is an incredible amount of risk in following your dreams, so people's instinct is often to hedge their bets. But that hedge keeps people from fully committing to their endeavors. Your deepest desires will take your deepest focus. "I realized that to have the level of success," Smith went on, "that I want to have, it's difficult to spread it out and do multiple things. It takes such a desperate, obsessive focus. You really have got to focus with all of your fiber and all of your heart and all of your creativity."

What I'm proposing in this book, and what Smith is alluding to, is that people are losing out on an opportunity to follow their dreams because it's ingrained in our society to play it safe and take the responsible route. We've convinced ourselves that such lofty expectations for our lives are, in fact, irresponsible. The argument of this book is to tell you the opposite. Putting all emotional benefits aside, we can use logic to choose our dreams over and over again. Plan A *is* the most reasonable choice.

A and B plans are not so different than penning a pros and cons list. Maybe you've made such a checklist to help determine which car to buy, what vacation to take, or what book to read. I would argue that you'd be hard pressed to find an instance in which you made a pros and cons list for a decision of huge significance in your life. Did you use a handy pros and cons list to choose your spouse? Your entire career path?

Where is the logic in splitting a piece of scrap paper down the middle and listing amenities on one side and liabilities on the other? It's merely a misguided attempt to be responsible. It's a concerted effort to be logical and guide decision making away from danger. What we're doing this for, after all, is to increase our potential. We're looking to maximize our opportunity and minimize our risks. But this isn't how we spark interest and passion in our lives. Take someone like professional surfer Kelly Slater, for example. He didn't become one of the greats after making a list. Slater has created purpose on that board. His decision came from a desire that didn't need pen and paper.

Consider that your peak expression must come from something more resilient than simply managing pros and cons. The drummer for the band Blink 182, Travis Barker, describes the opposite of a pros and cons list when talking about his head to toe tattoos and rock star life. Barker consciously tattooed most of his body at a young age to hedge against the risk of compromise. He figured with his body, including his neck and parts of his face, covered in tattoos he *had* to make it in music or face life with limited options. In his mind, it was music or nothing. Even for a man so committed, so willing to enroll in a life of deliberate practice, he made a permanent decision to provide a safeguard against the tug that we all feel to wise up and ditch our lofty goals. If Barker remained tattoo free and hit the bouts of adversity everyone endures, the pull of perceived safety and the socially reinforced norms of a regular job might well have overpowered his version of going right.

If quitting isn't an option then there's no reason even to let the idea enter your mind. When a quality employee, collaborative partner, or significant other come forward to express a desire to end the relationship, you have to determine whether or not to encourage this person to stay. In my opinion, there's no option but to support their desire to quit, even if they aren't sure.

My former college pitching coach has a knack for hard-nosed coaching. After a recent challenging day of conditioning, one of his young prospects came to him with concerns that this wasn't for him. Thinking he was going to have a back and forth dialogue with his coach, the athlete was surprised to hear his that it was his last day on the team. For the coach, one hint at quitting wasn't the start of a creative process. It was fate, and it was a death wish. How can a teammate with doubt contribute among a team of individuals single-mindedly focused on the game?

CHAPTER 3

SCAFFOLDING

GOING RIGHT IS the process of claiming our name in lights. It's living our fantasies and pursuing our wildest dreams. This is not, however, a matter of simple realization and overnight success. It's a process. And, like most serious endeavors, support and encouragement are crucial to success. The scaffolding built around this kind of decision-making is critical for the construction of a going right experience. The concepts that make up this scaffolding are basic tenets and practices. They are not necessarily in chronological order. Each is important on their own, but each one is not required to make going right a reality. It's possible to employ this scaffolding and still not execute the right approach. They are merely supporting structures that aid in peak human expression.

A WILLINGNESS TO ACCEPT NEGATIVE FEEDBACK

A willingness to receive negative feedback is one of the critical attributes for going right. It is, simply, best described as having a growth mindset. This term was coined by renowned author and Stanford psychologist Carol Dweck in her book *Mindset*. Dweck is the pioneering researcher on two general worldviews, fixed and growth mindsets.

While criticism may be difficult to take, it is essential to understanding and internalizing where you need to improve.

At the core of Dweck's work is the notion that we generally believe one of two things when we view ourselves. Fixed mindset individuals think that our characteristics are unchangeable attributes. A good example of this thinking is the idea that successful athletes are simply physically talented. They are successful at one thing because they're good at one thing. And their skill set does not enable them to excel in other areas, such as music. This mindset views attributes as unchangeable characteristics, so the consequences are seemingly greater to succeed in a particular field.

A growth mindset views our attributes as malleable traits that we can develop (or degrade) through our own choices and actions. In a growth mindset, skills and intelligence can be learned through practice and study. Anyone can succeed as long as they put their mind to it.

Personal attributes should always be viewed as malleable and transferrable. And negative feedback or criticism should be absorbed and used to facilitate necessary changes. Being able to internalize and accept this information on face value is incredibly important for going right. It isn't human nature to get feedback and immediately go to refine the process. But building your decision-making process with that in mind will make you an improved person. It supports and contributes to navigating failures and adversity along the way. And, it's ammunition to continually improve.

COMMUNITY

A community of support around you is a vital part of the scaffolding necessary to embrace the going right. Life is not lived in a bubble. It is inherently social—at work, home, or at leisure—and a community of people, along with their encouragement and the examples they set can be incredibly influential. Community is more than the mere presence of other people. It's about filling your life with people who support your peak expression. The people are the ones who will push and prod and encourage you to take the extra step, who will lead by example, and who will find strength in others' success.

Given that virtually none of us live our lives in solitude, we all have a community to some degree. Some of us choose our community, others are given their community, and many exist in a combination of both. An unsupportive community will encourage you to compromise. A supportive one will aid in our decision making, our perception of success, and our individuality. If anyone is going to take on the mantle of going right in relationships, career, and lifestyle, a community will be instrumental in supporting the cause.

PURPOSE

Purpose and our choices surrounded it, is a key driver to going right. Purpose not only gives us meaning and direction, but it also provides context for our what we value most. Purpose is the underlying foundation of our most important decisions. Purpose keeps us in pursuit of our ultimate goals.

Purpose, however, is not motivation. It is not an emotional tug of the heartstrings. Long and arduous pursuits require discipline, which is the ability to continue without the presence of motivation. It is the longer lasting, more reliable source for going right decision making. It's your connection to purpose that will transcend surface-level drivers like motivation, external praise, or reward.

IMMERSION

Ready. Set. Go. Like any pursuit, it's important to realize that much of the manifestation comes in *doing*. We hear this time and time again when it comes to entrepreneurship. Some of the best advice I ever received in business was, "You'll never be ready. Start!" I can't emphasize this enough. Far too many people get stuck in the whiteboarding phase because they believe they must plan and analyze everything. Your ducks will never be in a row! Your watertight plan is out of date the moment you finish it.

Immersion requires getting your hands dirty immediately. No one reaches their desired outcomes as an outside observer. Paralysis by analysis is a real thing, and the best remedy is a dose of dirty work. Start the project, ask the girl out, sign up for that first guitar lesson already. I hate to sound all Nike about it, but just do it.

To begin any endeavor, you just start. Along the journey, you improvise, adapt, and overcome. Our baseball team at the University of San Diego had a sports psychologist, Karlene Sugarman, who would often reinforce the idea of process. You put the big, result oriented, goals on the wall and dive in. The process is being immersed in the craft, in the discipline of doing. It's the early morning strength training. It's the midday studying to uncover more scholarship opportunities. It's in the afternoon practices carving out a skill set better than your peers. None of this can happen at the whiteboard or in a goal-setting meeting. This all happens in the mix with hands dirty, toiling with the craft.

INVENTION VS. INNOVATION

Last but not least, a key support structure for going right is a power move that resides in knowing the difference between invention and innovation. World-renowned powerlifter and strength coach, Louie Simmons, put it best by saying, "I didn't invent toilet paper, but I'm smart enough to use it."

Not to knock some of the world's great inventions, but innovation is about stimulation, using your community, your ingenuity, and your creativity to create a better environment. As we look for ways to live a going right life, we want to build on the groundwork that exists. Innovation can increase progress by piggybacking on foundational developments and learning from past failures, while invention would likely retrace the processes and failures of history to surpass it.

These support structures are helpful tools on your utility belt when grabbing hold of the going right life. Like any utility belt, the tools won't do the job for you. This process can be an arduous journey, and it helps, as any substantial trek, to pack accordingly. The context of this decision-making effort should reflect a lifetime of thousands of tiny decisions to embrace going right rather than one, single spark that will set in motion a life of resulting action. We must be prepared to be diligent in our decision making time and time again. When we decide to tackle a going right approach, we need to understand the work is just beginning.

Along this road to explain what exactly going right looks and feels like, it's also vital to examine identity and development. There is a mountain of exciting work being done by leading academics on adult development. Adult development refers to a contemporary understanding that human consciousness develops not just up until adulthood, but continues throughout life. Up until the 1950s and 1960s, much of the current research was focused on child development and adolescent maturation. Swiss psychologist Jean Piaget, who worked in the early part of the 20th century, came up with the theory of cognitive development called 'genetic epistemology.' It laid the groundwork for future generations surrounding the cognitive development of children.

Piaget's work set the stage for additional exploration into post-adolescent advancement, which is now a major focal point in positive psychology. This is a relatively new academic field that concentrates on solving the riddles of psychological disorders by enabling people to thrive through performance, flow states, and adult development.

Fifty years ago psychology focused on pathologies. It would have been, back then, taboo to consult a psychologist about improving your golf game. The psychology shelf at your local bookstore is now chock full of books on improving all aspects of your game—including your short game—from insights to happiness to advanced consciousness for performance and general well-being. Numerous Fortune 500 companies rely on the work of psychologists to properly hire, organize, and develop their employees cognitively. Sports teams have full-time psychologists to help athletes mentally prepare for games. Many Americans are actively seeking altered states via psychedelic drugs and medicines. In progressive Venice Beach, where I live, I often hear about ayahuasca ceremonies and controlled DMT experiences.

Throughout this book, we'll revisit the developmental implications of going right. And, no, this approach doesn't require conforming to increased popular interest and experimentation in psychedelics. But these trends do indicate a groundswell in the potential value and true importance of cognitive development. After all, people, organizations, and entire communities have malleable characteristics relative to their stages of development that are affected by our decision making.

I'm going to focus on a body of research work called Constructive Developmental Framework (CDF) to help us guide this discussion about of how we evolve through specific adult stages and mark the progress of our conscious development. CDF was created by Robert Kegan, a developmental psychologist, and author who taught at Harvard for more than four decades. The adult stages of development can be complex and, to that end, I'm going to try to spell out a clear, sufficient understanding of what it means to advance to mature stages of consciousness.

It's an odd concept that our conscious minds stagnate when we reach adulthood and that stages of development are only for children. Yet that was the scientific approach for many generations. Nowadays we're more comfortable with the idea that life is an ever-expanding web of complexity and that we continue to grow and mature and learn. This process is a natural evolution as we transcend and include our past. The words "transcend" and "include" are vital to understanding adult development, which is best described as a set of Russian nesting dolls. Earlier, simpler stages are representative of the smaller dolls. Subsequent stages of conscious development are symbolized by ever larger dolls. Each doll, like a more evolved conscious mind, includes the previous levels (or stages). It includes the former self but transcends it as well. As the mind develops and expands, it grows and holds all prior stages and iterations. More advanced conscious minds are more complex and can hold more than smaller, previous stages can.

There is a strong case to be made that advanced stages of adult development will help with the ability to navigate life's inexorable challenges. A higher level of consciousness has a utilitarian value to those interested in pursuing lofty goals.

What is consciousness exactly? Yuval Noah Harari, an Israeli historian, professor in Jerusalem, and the author of several books on human history, including "Sapiens," describes consciousness as the mind's framework for navigating subjective experiences. Humans have consciousness, and robots do not because we, as sentient beings, feel and crave. It's the sensation and desire that defines consciousness. When it comes to what drives our decision making, it turns out that our consciousness can shape everything about our mental processes.

The particular stages of our development can affect how we view what motivates us. To understand motivation, we must understand what the mind values. We need to know where we believe value comes from. These values shape our sensations and our desires. Our consciousness can create value out of our desires.

Ron Heifetz, the founder of the Center for Public Leadership, an academic research center at Harvard, and an expert and author on leadership studies, has examined the critical differences between technical and adaptive challenges. In his book "Leadership Without Easy Answers," a technical problem is an issue solved by experts. For example, a doctor treating a broken bone. Adaptive challenges, however, require new learning. The solutions in these cases have no definitive answer. For example, tackling the medical profession's ever-increasing dependence on opioid prescriptions is an adaptive challenge for which there is no clear answer. In many adaptive challenges, it's often difficult to discern precisely what the problem is. Adaptive challenges are solved through evolution. People and perspectives and ideas must change to solve them. Most people are affected by both technical and adaptive challenges. What often trips us up on our journeys, however, is when we attempt to solve adaptive challenges with technical means. This will never work because what we need is adaptation. This is where conscious adaptation has critical importance for us.

Early adult stages of consciousness can't comprehend and solve more complex adaptive challenges. More mental complexity brings with it a broader framework through which to examine more solutions. This complexity brings advantages for a person in navigating their struggles in complex personal relationships, work, and various aspects of life.

As we evolve into later stages of consciousness, we are able to trade black and white dogma for layers of understanding, like peeling an onion. Advanced development can alter an individual frame of perspective. Consider that anything that challenges our assumptions breaks our existing developmental framework and is a catalyst for progressive adult development. We're living in a world with a significant scarcity of later stage minds and getting more people to undertake a going right approach will be a compelling provider for more committed, deeply focused, potential maximizing, skill-transferring people. It's a prescription for moving the needle on our own conscious evolution. Going right not only has many tangible utilitarian advantages, but it also comes with a remarkable bonus in the form of conscious development.

While there are many different theories of adult development, the Constructive Development Framework is arguably the most comprehensive. Kegan's construction of the developmental process outlines a series of stages. The age ranges associated with these stages are generalizations. And many adults, it should be noted, will never develop into the highest stages. Most issues in our lives that challenge our limits occur at our edge of conscious development where we are stuck between one stage and evolving to the next.

STAGE ONE: THE IMPULSIVE MIND

The first stage and is most associated with the mind of early childhood. The simplicity of this conscious mind has just a single point of understanding, falls back on natural impulses, and is unable to question or identify self. In this stage, life is a series of all-consuming impulsive reactions to hunger, fatigue, and attention. When a baby is hungry, all of reality is hunger. There is no conscious space for other complexity for the baby to understand that she is a self who is hungry or that there are other people who have different feelings. This stage has a somewhat archaic structure, as it is consciousness with zero dimensions.

STAGE TWO: THE IMPERIAL MIND

Like all stages in this construct, this one transcends and includes the former stage. The Imperial Stage includes the Impulsive Mind. This stage, like its aggressively egotistical name, is defined by being self-aware. Yet people at this stage are still unable to imagine another point of view. The experience through one's own eyes *is* the experience. At a very young age, most of us learn to identify as a sentient being with unique traits, desires, and a worldview we can claim as our own.

This level of consciousness sends and receives information solely to get needs met. At this stage, the individual will follow rules because motivation stems, not from belief in the rules, but in self-preservation. A child at this stage will choose not to steal a toy from a friend not because she believes stealing is wrong, but avoiding the punishment associated from stealing. This often doesn't last long, however, because most consciousness evolves to understand through contact and conflict that other people have opinions and needs as well. Remember, experiences that challenge our assumptions break our current mental frame. The very notion that our experiences are different allows the mind to denote multiple perspectives.

STAGE THREE: THE SOCIALIZED MIND

The next stage is made possible when guiding principles are introduced as a way to deal with ours, and others', needs. It's here we observe plurality. Think about what structures, such as rules, laws, and religion can do to provide solutions for our needs. They are a convenient lens for managing decisions. We often call these institutional principles values. When people reach a certain level of social maturity, they identify the importance of these guiding frameworks. At this stage that we recognize the needs of others, we develop a conscious, experience guilt, and can express empathy. I distinctly remember moving into this stage as a young athlete. I suddenly claimed qualities such as discipline, honesty, and professionalism because of my allegiance to the institution of high-level baseball. I not only began to believe in the importance of these values, I demanded my own loyalty to them.

The Socialized Mind is the most common level of development in adults today. It's generally a follower oriented mindset because these individuals send and receive information through the lens of external social structures. Without yet developing a unique personal charter, Socialized Minds are predictably in alignment with the values set forth for them by their geography, family, political party, and so on. This would explain the increasingly polarizing dynamic of the political landscape.

STAGE FOUR: THE SELF-AUTHORING MIND

This stage emerges as the self is able to break the socialized framework. When a person is able to hold a truth that is counter to their socialized allegiances, they are able to transcend the boundaries of that allegiance. For example, the self-authoring Catholic transcends and includes their Socialized Mind when they believe disconfirming information about the Catholic dogma and authors their own belief structure.

The namesake of this stage describes the individual's ability to get enough distance from their social confines. These individuals begin to see outside the bounds of the frame of each social structure. This kind of consciousness can entertain discursive thought. This mind can look at both sides of an argument as well a more foundational truth. The limitations of this stage are that these individuals send and receive information in the world that support their personal agenda. They create their own dogma in doing so which opens up a resistance to disconfirming information and result in some blind spots.

STAGE FIVE: THE SELF-TRANSFORMING MIND

Kegan argues that the bell curve of humanity today does not evolve beyond stage four, but a small number of people do. This final stage of conscious evolution and development is built around the idea that we, as individuals, can see multiple ways to be correct, seek justice, and show fairness. This level of complexity is extremely rare and advances the ability to recognize and hold true opposite perspectives and contradictions. This stage gives up the need to defend correctness and personal views, but rather is fluid, like a living organism acting and reacting to the interplay happening around it. This mindset can look back on previous ideologies and connect the dots between them rather than view them as individual islands separate from one another.

The Self-Transforming mind is also referred to as the balcony view. It offers enough space to see the world as a series of systems, including the ability to see the self and its biases. This stage of consciousness can get enough distance from our own dogma to see our filter at work in the world. Someone with this level of social maturity can balance mainstream viewpoints and rebellious opinions simultaneously. They're able to create an argument both for and against a controversial proposition. They are open to the idea that there are grey areas in life. This stage both values and is critical of any one stance. Furthermore, this mindset is often found seeking information that challenges the systems it observes.

The further we push our own authentic efforts in going right, the more meaningful our pursuits will become. Taking this path will cultivate a framework that can support developmental evolution to these high-level stages where individuals will be able to view their surroundings with a birds-eye view. At this point, people can see the movement of individuals, the rhythm of social situations, and the interplay of personalities. This is the underlying concept that the depth of our experiences and the increasing stakes of pursuing them to our fullest are significant catalysts for general development through these stages of consciousness, and which will continue to show up in our conversation about going right.

→　→　→

When I look back on my own development, I can see that I was able to connect with and maintain a particular goal: mastery of baseball. I evolved dramatically between the time I told my dad I wanted to play professional baseball and the first paycheck I received for playing. Not only did I look, feel, and perform differently on a baseball field across a span of nearly twenty years, my consciousness was different. Pursuing peak expression drives conscious development in ways that cannot be replicated otherwise. Going right moves that needle.

Interestingly, there's a spiral-like effect to conscious development, where people evolve to a specific capacity only to circle back to a similar (but different) place, then challenge previous assumptions just to catapult into a new arena, with new skills and perspectives. As for me, thankfully I've transcended my playing career. If all I became was a socialized view of myself as an athlete, I would never be able to transcend. Anything that challenges assumptions breaks the existing developmental frame. Refusing to challenge assumptions keeps people stuck. Going right will guarantee forward progress.

Soon we will discuss the tried and true justifications for going right. The next chapters will focus on the black and white, un-avoidable utilitarian advantages of doing so. It's in this discussion that we will dive into the inevitable struggle(s) people face when they embrace this approach. We feel like we are risking more by chasing these dreams. The stakes feel higher. There are fewer safety nets. All of these feelings are understandable. The grav-ity of this perceived struggle, then, puts a premium on purpose. When you're on the long road to mastery and excellence, you're bound to confront failure, poverty, adaptive challenges, and un-foreseen adversity.

Onward!

CHAPTER 4

WHICH VERSION OF YOUR STORY ARE YOU TELLING YOURSELF?

WHILE STANDING AT the crossroads of any meaningful decision, we have a choice. Move towards a more actualized self or sacrifice your true being. Fear of failure is the leading motivator of not taking the going right route. Fear is a legitimate, and understandably frightening, emotion, yet it's lost on most people that we're often working with faulty or wrong information. So in an effort to be logical, let me be the first to tell you that fear is likely showing up because you don't have all the facts.

Hear me out.

In any decision or risk analysis, we're often focused on what the positive and negative outcomes will be. We are almost always inclined to avoid a negative result. Whether we actually *are* acting in our best interest or not, we think we are. Only a psychopath would intentionally choose a detrimental outcome, right?

One of the odd ways we look at decision making—both our own and other peoples'—is that we often highlight our own failures, and downplay our successes, while emphasizing other people's achievements and ignoring their failures. Risk analysis is dictated by the viewer. We don't see the shortcomings inside the stories we perceive as apparent successes. It may tickle our fancy to hear that Michael Jordan didn't make his freshman high school basketball team, but we leave it at that. It's a cute fact with a cliche lesson within a larger narrative that we already know. That's the narrative fallacy at work. We know the Michael Jordan story ends *really* well. It's an endearing anecdote in a world of basketball and business greatness. But to fifteen-year-old Michael Jordan, the adversity and uncertainty of that moment were real. When he went home from school that day, he probably felt like a failure. He was scared in the same way we all get scared.

Which version of your story are you telling yourself? It's a compelling exercise for everyone to do. Nobody achieved the highlight reel version of their own story without considerable failure. Seeing each life story for what it is—a series of ups and downs—is an essential part of our perspective on decision making. If we had the full understanding of the tethered relationship that success has with failure, we would fear it less. When you examine any seemingly obvious success story, it's terribly two-sided. When we observe success stories in people, it's important to bear in mind that we are seeing them in reverse. Conversely, we experience our own successes and failures in real time.

The reason you've heard of brands and their tales such as

Nike is that it won. Even if you dig into Nike's history—clearly a winning brand— our interpretation of their various pitfalls are clouded. In fact, they don't seem like failures at all from our perspective. In Nike's case, you can't unknow the multi-billion dollar grand finale.

When you look at the story of Phil Knight and Nike in order, from beginning to end, it is an absolute horror story. Like Michael Jordan, Knight reflected in his memoir "Shoe Dog" that "getting cut from my high school baseball team had been one of the greatest hurts of my life." We glamorize a few tales of adversity. We love hearing about legendary University of Oregon track coach, Bill Bowerman, making running soles with his waffle iron. We glamorize Steve Prefontaine running with Swooshes on his feet into immortality. We relish the intimacy of seeing Nike go from back of the Studebaker-type sales operation in the Pacific Northwest to a billion-dollar empire. The real story, however, isn't so pretty.

In the early days of the business, Knight recounts in his book, he took countless trips to Japan, most of which were fruitless. The company resembled more of a blindfolded game of pin-the-tail-on-the-donkey than a bonafide brand. Knight initially began what amounted to a distribution deal where he got the rights to sell a Japanese shoe company in California. When the Japanese executives asked what the name of his distribution company was, Knight, panicked and said, "Blue Ribbon." From 1962 to nearly 1971 Blue Ribbon served as an un-exclusive middle man between Japan and the American market. Those years were most notable for breached contracts, lawsuits, and not a single profitable year. Banks wouldn't lend him money, the FBI even came sniffing around, and his reputation was in tatters. Was it worth it? That's an easy question to answer when you know how it ends. Imagine being a young Phil Knight trying to answer that question with any amount of enthusiasm. Even the eventual name wasn't easy. Knight wanted to call it Dimension Six but at the eleventh hour, needing to send their new manufacturing partner a name—an employee suggested Nike, referencing the Greek goddess of victory. They scribbled it on the transcript and submitted their product order. If you thought the world's largest sports brand was a well thought out master plan, think again.

Whether you view this story as rife with failure or giddy with success, both are *true*. Even in 1978 when the world was watching Nike taking over a viable threat to the perennial sports shoe and apparel powerhouse—everywhere you turned there were swooshes—all was not so rosy. Knight put it bluntly in his memoir when he confessed that "industry watchers pointed to our new factories, and our sales, and said we were unstoppable. Few imagined we were broke. Or that our head of marketing was wallowing in a depression."

Sometimes the illusion is everything. While Nike was bringing in millions in revenue, they couldn't call themselves a success. People weren't aware that Nike had ten thousand dollars to its name, was floated fully by aggressive financing, and had received an injunction from the U.S. Treasury Department for $25 million in unpaid taxes. It's important to remember that in real time the road to success doesn't feel like happily ever after. Knight pointed out that "amid all this turmoil, amid all this uncertainty about the future, we needed a morale booster." Nike would win its battles and go on to dominate the sports world. And all those hardships are quickly forgotten.

Try to put this thinking in the context of your own life. I do this often when I look back because anyone can describe my story as a start-to-finish story of perfect swishes. Little league? It wasn't even close. I was probably considered the best player in our league's history. I remember being pulled out of class in grade school to take special tests to evaluate me intellectually. "That would explain your work," they said. Middle school? Class president. By then I was already a force on the international baseball scene. High school? I broke the game. Varsity letterman as a freshman, earned All-State honors my senior year while courting a dozen scholarships from Division I programs. I ranked in the top five in my class academically all four years. I negotiated with Major League Baseball teams—and did my math homework at the same time—telling them why they needed to sign me to a mid-six-figure deal. While my classmates stressed through their senior year, I had already signed my National Letter of Intent to the University of San Diego on scholarship. Once there I walked onto campus and stole the catcher's position from an All-American, and went on to win most valuable player as a freshman in Fall Camp. I don't think I made a single out as a batter until the last day of the first semester. Over the next few years, I earned numerous 1st Team All-Conference honors and multiple Conference Championships spearheading a Top 25 NCAA program into a 4th Ranked National Powerhouse. And I was drafted by the hometown San Diego Padres to play professional baseball.

Even after I ended my baseball career, I co-founded two successful businesses before the age of thirty. I competed in the CrossFit Games and the Strongman National Championships. I run a highly successful traveling international seminar, manage a salaried writing career, and have a beautiful wife who's more successful than I am.

Sounds like a dream, right? While that story is all true, it's poignantly selective. I could tell another right side that would be full of perennial failures.

The truth is I grew up as a shy and skinny kid. I was petrified of public speaking. I cried in front of my fourth class, unable to recite the Halloween poem. And then continued to cry repeatedly throughout grade school, middle school, and high school. I wasn't accepted into the first high school I applied to (I cried in the interview). I initially wanted to play baseball at Stanford, but found myself on crutches on a recruiting trip and playing second fiddle my best friend, Randy Molina. Then I set my sights on Georgia Tech only to get a follow-up email from the coach after my tour from the coach which said: "You're a D1 catcher, kid, but we're picking a Georgia kid, instead."

I ended up with several college scholarship offers at far less sexy programs. *No problem.* When the University of San Diego baseball coach, Eric Valenzuela, sat down with me and my dad in our dining room he calmly explained that they'd love to have me play for the school but "we're out of money," he said. "I just signed a junior college first baseman, and we're out of scholarships. But I did investigate, and your grades qualify for this academic scholarship."

When I joined the team in the fall, I immediately discovered the placard of Kevin Hoffmockel, the best catcher in San Diego.

I knew I had to beat out an All-American, but I thought I was the only competition. How many catchers did they bring in?

Sophomore year I signed up to play in the Cape Cod League, a summer league for college players that is often a staging ground for future Major Leaguers, only to have the offer revoked at the end of the regular season. I went undrafted as a junior. As a senior, I had the worst statistical season in the most crucial year of my playing career. I eventually was drafted, but not until thirty-fifth round. Waiting through the first thirty-four rounds was interminable. I sat in my parents' backyard with my girlfriend—who would leave me within a year—not knowing what to do if my name was never called.

In my first two seasons as a professional baseball player, I felt like a foreigner on the field. My once prized throwing arm became a liability. I feared throwing the ball back to the pitcher instead of as a viable threat behind the plate. When you're a professional athlete, no one wants to hear anything out of your mouth other than gratitude, and they don't want to see anything other than starry eyes. I drank more than I should as a professional athlete. At times there were more drinks than hits. While playing for the Lake Elsinore Storm, a single A affiliate for the Padres, I got the "San Diego Padres no longer need your services" talk over the phone. *That's it.*

Success is fully tethered to failure. And vice versa. Yet it's only failure that is guaranteed. It's guaranteed even if you're not vulnerable enough to give your best effort. You can't hide from it. If we're all going to struggle, it seems that we ought to at least struggle in the places that make us better doing the activities that bring us joy with the people that help us grow.

→ → →

One winter in between baseball seasons, I lived in a small apartment in Culver City, CA. While doing some off-season training to prepare for my first spring training, I made extra money working in the back of a shoe factory scanning shoes and filling boxes.

My effort, like everything I worked at, was 110%. When I punched in, I meant business. I went to work at a blistering pace. I never wanted to be seen resting or lacking in a genuine work ethic. I built cardboard shipping boxes twice as fast as anyone else. I even developed a system enabled me to scan exponentially faster than the way I was initially trained.

My efforts didn't go unnoticed. My manager, Javier, spoke to me one day, not to applaud my efforts but to get me to fall in line with the way everyone else worked.

"Calm, Logan," Javier said. "There will always be shoes."

For a moment it gave me a sense of relief. I'd earned both my paycheck and the respect of the factory workers. On the other hand, in the several weeks, I'd been busting my ass in the back of the factory, I hadn't made a discernible dent into shoes. Was he right? Everything I understood told me that more is better and that slacking off would get me nowhere. I could keep this pace forever, and the business would benefit by doing more work faster. Was my math wrong?

I thought about Javier's message on the way home that day. *Would there always be shoes?* In the subsequent years, that same company has subsequently downsized by half, and likely won't survive the next three years. There, most literally, won't always be shoes.

The implications of this cautionary tale are important, but they not for the reasons you might think. There's no guarantee my additional work would help the business survive. But that doesn't mean Javier was right. He took a certain number of observations of the past and made a generalist determination about the future. This story is critical before we move forward into this decision-making model. Safety is a story we tell ourselves. Javier likely understood, based on past experience, that he was safe at his job. This is critical because this perceived safety is often misused as a justification for conceding the effort of pursuing our peak expression.

Too many individuals are guided by poor information in their decision making. We often opt for security and don't take the route that would be our true selves. We believe that there will always be shoes. The man I met on the plane, John, reminded me to keep playing baseball because he knew the somber reality of giving up your best self. Javier had the same belief. The future was relatively safe and predictable until it wasn't. What we will see in the coming chapters is that since there *won't* always be shoes, that we ought to maximize our ability to contribute to our best self and others with meaningful work and passionate pursuits. The illusion that we can give this up for some sort of certainty is a myth. The only certainty is uncertainty.

→ → →

Societal pressure pushes us to avoid going right by painting it as an irresponsible choice. We are guided to relieve ourselves of the overwhelming duty we have to pursue purpose. Even worse yet, we often look at passionate drive as crazy.

One of the more recognizable special forces soldiers is a man named David Goggins. He was the only US warfighter to receive the Navy SEAL trident, complete Army Ranger training, and US Air Force special operations qualifications. Goggins, who is black, grew up in an abusive home and sat behind the local Ku Klux Klan leader's son in class. His life was peppered with trauma. He had a stutter, weighed close to 300lbs, and finished second to last, academically, in his high school class. Yet Goggins went on to an extensive special operations career, completed what is arguably the most demanding military training, BUD/S, three times, owns a world record for the most pull-ups in 24-hours (more than 4,000!), and has a notable ultra-Marathon career. In a recent podcast interview ultra-marathoner and author Rich Roll, Goggins described the socialized demonization of going right: "When you're passionate, they think you're crazy. You can't even explain to people why you're doing it or why you did what you did because you found your purpose and once you find your purpose you can't really explain it to normal people because they don't understand passion. They live everyday life just going, not really finding their purpose. I've become a foreign language to people, so they put me in this category of, You're just crazy. No, no, no. I'm passionate. I've found my purpose in this life."

Pursuing purpose looks different for everyone. As a coping mechanism, we tend to make these natural urges dangerous, out of reach, or, in Goggin's case, "crazy." It's this concession that is the biggest mistake. We set ourselves up by believing that the logical thing to do is to realize that our dreams are unrealistic emotions run amok, and the smart thing to do is to be something else.

CHAPTER 5

THE COSMIC CALENDAR

WHAT WE'RE DIVING into is why we, as humans, consistently choose to be less effective, less successful, less happy than we can, and want to be. Most Americans will choose exactly what they don't want with their lives—in their relationships, careers, and their self-expression— through a litany of small concessions. We are, by some measure, turning large groups of young, motivated, bright-eyed youth with big dreams turn into dull, unfulfilled, unremarkable people. It's a nearly ubiquitous mindset in today's modern framework that the logical approach to life is to go to college, get a decent job, work hard at a desk, have a family, but never to risk it all and strive for greatness. After all, we can't all be Beyonce.

The full, honest pursuit of what we really want in life is often viewed as reckless, unrealistic, and irrational. We're following a well-trodden path because it's smart to do so. To best understand where this behavior comes from we need to understand our origins. Humans have been a work of evolutionary process for more than 2.5 million years.

People are more than our nationalities, languages, and cultural norms. This is so much deeper than tendencies toward conservative or liberal, Christian or Muslim, organized or sloppy. This is a matter of looking at human history in context. Take the Cosmic Calendar, for example, a pedagogical tool which shrinks 13.8 billion years (the age of our universe) into a single calendar year. On this calendar, the Big Bang takes place at midnight on January 1, and the eve of December 31 is this current moment. In this shrunken view of history, humans discovered fire sixteen minutes ago. Agriculture? Twenty-Eight seconds ago. In fact, we can fit the last 437.5 years into the last second. Our modern understanding of the world and humanity fits in a second, meaning we're much more alike than we think. I don't mention this just so we all can get along (though we should). I bring it up because many of the hard and fast truths that we use as guiding principles are quite flimsy when examined carefully.

I wouldn't be the first person to suggest that the comforts of modern life have essentially halted evolution. We do have a host of problems and pain points these days, but it's not terribly challenging to live long enough these days to have a child. For the bulk of our evolutionary existence, procreation and life was fraught with overcoming the natural elements, food scarcity, and an extraordinarily short life expectancy. The fact that you have time to read these words and question things like the meaning of your life assumes things we couldn't assume centuries ago: that we'll all likely survive the night and have food and shelter secured indefinitely. That comfort is new.

As humans, we're biologically adapted to survive. Stress and risk are warning signs of death and are evolutionarily disadvantageous. We are naturally inclined to avoid these as they are the very habits that would keep us alive long enough to procreate in our evolutionary past. Yet what I've begun to propose with the going right approach is that we have a systemic problem when we avoid uncertainty and seek to minimize risk. What we have here is a life's biggest prank on humanity. Humans have developed an existence where most of the things that kept us alive in our past are currently diminishing us.

Consider the pace which our environment has evolved. While humans have been fumbling around for 2.5 million years, we've only recently settled into homes. Having an inventory of food is a novelty. These days we're used to a rapidly changing technology environment, but it's helpful to remember how much time humanity has spent in an extremely different world. In many ways, our brain's software is developed for a different landscape. It took us 2,494,000 years to invent the wheel. Yet in the last 115 years, we've gone from rudimentary airplane flight to interplanetary space travel. In the past thirty years alone we've evolved the telephone from a glorified two-way radio to a supercomputer that has access to nearly universal information at the touch of a button.

It's important to recognize the evolutionary pieces that are relevant to us today. While we feel the natural pull to seek safety and avoid uncertainty for survival reasons, our DNA also seeks human connection and meaning. Our evolution rewards behavior that has our biology in mind. Sex feels good. Playing with fire doesn't. Quenching your thirst in the heat of the day is satisfying, while going without food sets off painful alarms in the body.

Similarly, we thirst for social connections and shared purpose because for most of our existence isolation was extremely dangerous. Interpersonal relations are as much a driver of evolution as simple survival. Our ability to band together, share empathy, and coordinate our efforts actually increases our viability as a species. After all, we didn't get to the top of the food chain because of our muscles. These advantages drove the development of language, currency, security, and, as a result, massive human movements that would become armies and even empires.

As you can tell, our biology is in a bit of tug-o-war with itself. Our DNA wants us to survive above and beyond everything else, because in our world survival and inevitably procreation pays off. The trouble is the important signals of fear that stem from our biology's desire to survive can send us running from our purpose. At the same time, the pleasure we receive from overcoming challenges, pursuing purpose, and sharing our accomplishments with the world are, at times, at odds with what's safe and known. When the fear-based side of our DNA is winning, we're in real trouble.

→ → →

At a young age, we begin to learn a basic understanding of time and mortality. Once we understand that life doesn't last forever, we start the life-long process of framing up how we'd like to spend the short time we all have on earth.

These attempts to carve out an identity and a path often take years to formulate, are rife with ups and downs, and are never fully complete. But it is a nearly universal feeling of responsibility. Questions about the meaning of life and how we should spend it are always swirling through our minds, whether we're adolescents or adults, college baseball players or a reluctant software company employees on an airplane. Yet some people can't entirely take the initiative to make the necessary changes in their lives and decision making to find a more fulfilling life's work.

As we progress through our development, people often begin to mark their time and positions and allegiances with titles and names. We outline ourselves with phrases such as "I am a teacher" or "I am an athlete." Nate Helming, a well-known running and endurance coach in San Francisco, echoed this when he explained to me recently "Take runners for instance. First, as a runner, it's empowering. You say to yourself, 'I can run up that hill. I can complete that race. I don't need to take an Uber. Thank you. I'll just run there.'

"As you get more into it, you start reading the magazines, following the thought leaders of the sport, and wearing all the right gear. But, with the fuller assumption of that identity also comes with it the limitations of that community.

"Now you're saying, 'I'm a runner, so I probably shouldn't go skiing this weekend.. I might hurt myself.' or 'I'm a runner, so I can't help you move your couch over the weekend.'"

The more we understand the power of this socialized identity as well as its limitations, the more we can leverage it for the good while carving out our own path in this world.

Claiming identity is important—it empowers us—but ascribing ourselves as the embodiment of a profession doesn't give the full scope of who we are and what we aim to become. After all, it's the pursuit that matters most.

Like any captivating drama, there is always a conflict. The inner conflict of who we are and what we are becoming is the most important conflict in our lives. Finding purpose and having a clear mission is challenging, yes, but necessary for a fulfilling life. What is more critical than digging for a solution than that? Laundry?

We all have the ability to recognize and imagine idealism. Early philosophy used our capacity for idealistic thought as a clue to the existence of God. The mere fact that we could imagine perfection in an imperfect world meant there was a higher power.

As humans, we have the ability to understand, value, and imagine idealism, yet human nature is repeatedly characterized by our failings. Religion aside, it's a universal understanding that humans are flawed beings. Even when we try our best, one hundred percent of us are imperfect.

→ → →

Appealing to the emotional justification for going right does a poor job of getting people to follow through. It can also cause a few eye rolls. Isn't that the angle of every commencement speech, father/son pep talk, and motivational movie scene? There are a lot of people, like John, who suggest you should never settle while simultaneously settling themselves.

Emotional gestures spark motivation, but don't teach discipline. Motivation is the impetus that keeps us coming back to the project at hand. There are two main types of motivation, intrinsic and extrinsic. Intrinsic motivation is motivation that is fostered from within. This type of motivation is built on the premise that humans can evolve themselves. We can learn new skills and acquire reusable knowledge and that this process can be enjoyable. Intrinsic motivation occurs when the action itself fulfills a basic human need. The proximity of this motivation sources makes it difficult to shake and makes it a compelling driver of human activity.

Conversely, extrinsic motivation comes from outside of ourselves, often in the form of rewards or incentives. While extrinsic motivation is a common strategy for enticing human behavior in school, it's been found to be a far less effective motivator. The perception that extrinsic motivation is critical in scenarios, like school, is primarily based on the idea that humans don't enjoy learning and aren't compelled to do so on their own. This evolved into punishments for poor performance in schools, based on the assumption that students will do anything to avoid corporal punishment. It didn't take long to discover that human behavior is more affected by positive feedback, so shifts were made towards positive extrinsic motivation. Rewarding students for a job well-done yields better results than punishing them for less than satisfactory efforts. Yet, both forms of extrinsic motivation pale in comparison to the power of intrinsic motivation.

→ → →

The natural world is very different from the human one. Animals and plants and trees are biologically wired to make intrinsic decisions. Not many people can say the same. The clothes we wear, the food we eat, the environment we surround ourselves in, the jobs we chose, and many more things are extrinsically motivated. We express ourselves, in part, to satisfy external, socialized criteria.

The forces that push us to make decisions with an eye toward what our neighbors and friends think is best is conceding our true purpose and our best selves. Making more honest decisions—and accepting going right—elicits a more idealistic self.

On a fundamental level, we have a positive connotation with authenticity and a negative connotation with in-authenticity. Authenticity can be understood merely as truth. To be authentic is to express an accurate, objective understanding of a particular subject. Inauthenticity, on the other hand, is an expression of dishonesty. At best, it's an impersonation of something else. Yet we often fail to make decisions that are authentic even though we are telling ourselves otherwise. To fully understand going right, being authentic needs to have greater utility than being inauthentic.

Luckily, authenticity has tangible results. We love authentic partners more than inauthentic ones; we'd like to hire authentic employees before inauthentic ones; and artists authentic in their pursuits make better painting, music, poetry. But, why? To find the answer, we need to return to precisely what it means to be an authentic self. In an authentic expression, there is direct access to personal truth. In the inauthentic self, there is a disparity between what is true and what's being presented as true. Overcoming this gap takes work. Which brings to mind Oscar Wilde's oft-quoted maxim, "Be yourself; everyone else is already taken." The utility of authenticity is greater than that of inauthenticity because we just cannot impersonate better than an original.

In a classic study from the 1970s, Mark Lepper, David Greene, and Richard Nisbett observed the effect of extrinsic motivators in toddlers. The three researchers gave two groups of preschoolers who particularly enjoyed drawing the supplies and time to do so. One group, however, was told ahead of time that they would be given material rewards for their drawing efforts. Their prize was a certificate and a ribbon. The other group was not given a reward, nor were they told of such an arrangement ahead of time. While the unrewarded group continued to enjoy their drawing time and even produced increasingly better drawings weeks later, the rewarded group began to take less interest in drawing altogether. The implications of this indicate that the power of intrinsically motivated efforts can outpace extrinsically motivated efforts, but that extrinsic rewards can erode our intrinsic desires.

Matthew Crawford, a former Ph.D. student, turned think tank advisor turned motorcycle mechanic, writes about meaningful work in his book, "Shop Class as Soulcraft." Crawford says that "an external reward can affect one's interpretation of one's own motivation, an interpretation that comes to be self-fulfilling. A similar effect may account for the well-known fact that when someone turns a hobby into a business, he often loses pleasure in it. Likewise, the intellectual who pursues an academic career gets professionalized, and this may lead him to stop thinking."

What's the point of chasing intrinsic motivations if that utility includes such corrosive external rewards? Does success inevitably ruin a decision to go right? Crawford provides an important caveat. "You can earn money at something without the money, or what it buys, being the focus of your day," he says. "To be capable of sustaining our interest, a job has to have room for progress in excellence." And, just like that, we're precisely back on the road to going right. Get this wrong, and any decision to go right can evolve into an adverse decision.

When it comes to an original, authentic self we have to accept that within this approach are our highest goals. The pioneering mind behind the study of flow, Mihaly Csíkszentmihályi, sums up authentic decision making perfectly when he says in his book "Flow: The Psychology of Optimal Experience," "It doesn't matter what the choice is, as long as it is an expression of what the person genuinely feels and believes. Inauthentic projects are those a person chooses because they are what she feels ought to be done, because they are what everybody else is doing, and therefore there is no alternative. Authentic projects tend to be intrinsically motivated, chosen for what they are worth in themselves; inauthentic ones are motivated by external forces."

By not going right in relationships, work, and lifestyle to satisfy social norms and pressures, we're accepting inauthenticity. Csíkszentmihályi goes on to point out that "A similar distinction is that between *discovered* life themes when a person writes the script for her actions out of personal experience and awareness of choice; and *accepted* life themes when a person simply takes on a predetermined role from a script written long ago by others." A long journey of discovery is a useful tool in understanding the most accurate picture of authentic self.

The process of forging a unique path with many consecutive decisions to accept going right creates a rich environment to recognize a more accurate self. Not being authentic leaves us with less information, less feedback, and less opportunity to look at themselves. An honest awareness of oneself produces a clearer picture of our true self. And the commitment to going right, to any authentic project really, can compound our level of authenticity, which in turn compounds our ability to create value for others. Like anything, authenticity has its degrees. If we can understand that there are more abundant levels of authenticity, we can understand a scale of value. We can develop, especially with a growth mindset that sees opportunity in negative feedback, more and more value.

Accepting going right is a decision propagated by intrinsic motivations, which creates intrinsic satisfaction and is a closed loop system for development. We're motivated internally by choosing difficult, challenging, but purposeful pursuits and these come with the potential for clearly beneficial consequences. Remember our Navy SEAL friend, Goggins? He made the source of his motivation clear. "It was all internal. None of it was external," Goggins explained on the podcast. "I didn't care about money. I didn't care about wars. I didn't care about medals. I didn't care about Badwater. I don't care about ultra-running. These were all things for me to build the internal in myself... I did this to be proud of who I am as a human being. Most people live a lie, and I hated the lie I lived. The lie I lived was that I was nothing and I knew I was nothing. I wanted to be somebody and to be proud of who I was and move my life in that direction."

This journey has developmental benefits in addition to a potentially satisfying end result. When we examine the decision to do what others want us to do, we then have a relationship built on external, pre-destined motivations. This foundation doesn't allow for discovery to enrich the relationship and overall experience. A relationship such as this, Csíkszentmihályi writes in "Flow," would follow "accepted life themes," in Csíkszentmihályi's words, rather than the "discovered life themes, when a person writes the script for her actions out of personal experience and awareness of choice." Freedom of choice and a level of control on your own life's script is a necessary attribute of happiness, whereas to remain at the mercy of external forces creates an environment ripe for victimization. In that case, happiness is nearly impossible.

The path to authenticity cannot, by definition, be a path at all. To follow a pre-existing path would be characteristically inauthentic. The Spanish poet, Antonio Machado, put it best in this poem "Caminante no hay Camino:" "Traveler, there is no path, The path is made by walking..."

→ → →

Viktor E. Frankl, an Austrian neurologist and psychologist, Holocaust survivor, one of the originators of existential therapy, and the author of "Man's Search for Meaning," discussed the dynamic of idealism and realism at a talk he gave in Toronto in 1972. Frankl, who died in 1997, talks about the disparity between an ideal man and the "realistic" version of man in his talk. In the example, the majority of subjects in an experiment claimed their number one priority in life was to have meaning and purpose. A small subset said things such as money and security were their primary focus. Frankl then described a relevant corollary with airplanes.

Frankl asked the audience to imagine a starting and ending point—west to east on a straight horizontal axis—of a flight. He went on to describe that in a crosswind from the north, a pilot must use a technique called crabbing to avoid drifting to the south. The effect of this external force would send the plane below the desired destination. "You have to head for north of this airfield, and you have to fly that way, you see?" he explained, pointing out that the pilot needs to aim north of their desired destination to account for the wind. "This holds also for man," Frankl explained, relating the flight to the human struggle. "If you take man as he really is, we make him worse. But, if we overestimate him... If we seem to be idealists and overestimating, overstating man, looking at him that high, here above, you know what happens? We promote him to what he really can be. So, we have to be idealists in a way, because we then arrive at the true, real, realist. If you don't recognize a young man's will towards meaning, a search for meaning, you make him worse, you make him dull, you make him frustrated, you will add and contribute to his frustration, while if you presuppose in this man if in this, so-called criminal or juvenile delinquent or drug abuser, and so forth, there must be a so-called spark for search for meaning. Let's recognize this. Let's presuppose it and then you will elicit it from him and you will make him become what he's principally capable of becoming."

Frankl's view was that we can recognize our apparent fallibility and channel idealistic pursuits for self-actualization. Life brings a crosswind effect to every quest. To be realistic and curb our outlandish goals, we create flight plans that undershoot the realistic destinations we want in life. Even John, from the plane, isn't safe from the crosswind.

Most people choose to give up their dreams for more perceived practicality. If adults were able to tell their kindergarten-age self what they set out to be in life, their school-age self would almost always be disappointed. Why is that? We have polarized the notion of a good life and our true aspirations as opposites. On one side you have a logical path—safety and security and a repeatable script—and on the other, you have an emotional, risky dream. Taking this approach gives the impression that a life of passion and purpose cannot also have safety and security.

We may evaluate this transaction as a worthy trade-off. At someplace along the way, we justify giving up the thing we wanted most in life. A.G. Sertillanges, O.P., a French Catholic philosopher and spiritual writer in the early twentieth century, wrote, in "The Intellectual Life," "If you are compelled to earn your living, at least you will earn it without sacrificing, as so many do, the liberty of your soul. If you are alone, you will but be more violently thrown back on your noble purposes. Most great men followed some calling, plunge every day of your life into the spring with quenches and yet ever renews your thirst." We tell ourselves that deviating from our ideal life is smart and more realistic. But that is ignoring your true expression.

CHAPTER 6

YOU DOING YOU

THE WOMEN SURROUNDING me in my life are remarkably strong—both literally and figuratively— and empowered
individuals. Notably, my mom was the black sheep sibling that
ventured away from the herd. Societal norms were a force that
could not hold her in one place. She was born in Texas, but nei-
ther the state nor the country could contain her. She sought ad-
venture, and by age twenty she was living alone in Manhattan
Beach, CA flying internationally as a flight attendant for United
Air. She's still flying the "friendly skies" more than 45 years later.
During that time she has been to more countries than you can
count on all your fingers and toes in an industry that's gone from
glamour and respect to the somber post-9/11 state of bankrupt-
cies and cutbacks that the airline industry resides in now. In the

worst financial crisis of our lifetime, she saved the family financially while working for an industry hit as hard as any. This, of course, all managed with a smile on her face and a brief intermission to beat cancer.

My close friend Gabrielle Reece is a former international volleyball star, model, mother, tv personality, and entrepreneur. That list reads like the accomplishments printed on a book jacket (which she's also written!), but her best qualities are not found in search-engine descriptors. Gabby is a captivating individual, leader, and communicator. Aspiring leaders should study at her feet. She has the remarkable ability to read people with adept insightfulness, to empathize with astute clarity, and get to the heart of the matter with alacrity.

Gabby has the ability to produce through all facets of life. The choices she has made throughout her career are textbook examples of going right. She has done it over and over again, continually excelling and reinventing herself. Gabby is, in fact, the epitome of someone taking the principles of going right to heart. Her own experience and introspection led to curiosity. This curiosity turned to a passionate commitment. In her case, it began with volleyball.

Gabby's commitment enabled her to pursue her peak expression. The purpose she showed allowed her to develop her craft as a college athlete and ultimately as a professional, leading her volleyball team to tour around the world.

Gabby, who is 6'3", is an incredible all-around athlete. Not many people know that Gabby tried her hand at professional golf for a time. She committed four years of dedicated training to earn a place on the LPGA tour. It wasn't unlike Michael Jordan's stint in minor league baseball. From afar, it appeared as another decision in the vein of the going right approach, but it was not as simple as that. And it did not go as expected.

Pursuing professional golf was an honest effort on Gabby's part. It is also a great lesson in putting the cart before the horse. The process of going right is an evolution. Each iteration must transcend and include the previous stages. On paper, Gabby had all the ingredients for a successful transition to professional golf. She had an athletic foundation to meet or exceed that of her opponents. She had the time and the opportunity to learn the craft. Her fate, however, was sealed, as she is the first to admit when she approached the process with a level of disingenuousness. As an active sports professional, and a substantive career as a model, the golf idea began with the end-goal first. How do I get into the LPGA? Using an end goal is not a great way to start any endeavor. It's not a good idea to use the NBA as appropriate bait for young kids to start playing basketball, or to use a spot on the wall at the Metropolitan Museum of Art as an enticement for a young artist. Gabby didn't authentically learn to love golf first. Most LPGA stars start with clubs in their little kid hands because these are critical stages that professional athletes surely *transcend*, but most definitely *include*. What we observe is that you can't fake intrinsic motivation. It must be authentic because if anyone could get away with sorta-kinda being committed at a sport and still have success, her name would be Gabrielle Reece.

→ → →

Early in my amateur baseball days, I played a significant amount with an organization called Reviving Baseball in Inner Cities (RBI). RBI partnered with Major League Baseball and provided infrastructure and opportunities for baseball to thrive in urban and underprivileged areas.

There's a bit of self-selection that occurs with kids who choose to play a hundred baseball games each year. Not everyone's version dedication fits that mold. Part of going right involves some vetting of our impulses. We're often deceived in our journey to understand what gives us purpose and direction in our lives. Sometimes this trickery comes in the form of success, something which is extraordinarily common in sports. Young athletes who have a natural aptitude can be duped into thinking sports is their calling. Kids who can kick or throw the ball hard, or can shake a defender, feel good about their participation and they gain a false sense of superiority. Add to that the feeling of winning. Yet, without a purpose to connect to this type of surface level success, without deep, meaningful roots in the craft, the participation rarely lasts the test of time.

Athletics have a poignant emotional pull. It's this kind of extrinsic motivation, though, that can be misleading. And the pursuit will, in the long run, ebb when there is too much adversity and no purpose.

In 2001, a teammate on my RBI team, Dorell Wright, had every emotional reason in the world to continue his pursuit of playing in the Majors. Dorell was a warm, gregarious young kid with a big goofy smile from a bad neighborhood in South LA. We were just teenagers, but all of us had dreams of greatness. Almost half of that team would become professional baseball players. We were in an organization poised to make these dreams come true, *and* we were good enough, at this juncture, to do it.

Not only was Dorell good, but he also had upside. Upside is a word scouts use to describe projectability. He was good then, but people expected his best performances were yet to come. If he were a stock on the NASDAQ, he'd be a buy option. At 6'6", Dorell was, as one pro scout said to us, "All knees and elbows." Everyone saw greatness in Dorell.

Except Dorell.

Dorrell, as it turned out, had a greater interest in basketball. Our team was on a fast track to professional baseball, but Dorell's posture and general attitude was markedly unmotivated. While choosing one professional sport over another may seem negligible for an athletically gifted young man, it's important to understand the context. The smartest choice appeared to be to stay the course. Dorell would have certainly received a college scholarship, and likely be drafted into the MLB if he had only stayed the course. Dorell was also already in the conversation with a number of MLB scouts and college recruiters.

Baseball was the smart choice. But for Dorrell, his going right was to take the more difficult path and play basketball. To take this course, as he did, would demand his very best. Choices like this are seemingly, and the surrounding cultural influences tend to conspire against that choice. Coaches and parents and scouts all pleaded with Dorrell to "be smart." In Dorell's mind, the emotional tug towards baseball was not enough to propel a meaningful pursuit in it, no matter how many words of encouragement he received.

Dorell eventually quit baseball—along with the sure-fire path to a college scholarship and a likely professional contract—to focus on basketball. Developmentally, Dorell went from budding star to immediate intermediate. He had a decent high-school career in basketball but wasn't good enough to play in college. But he was driven, and he enrolled back in a prep school for a fifth year of high school. Dorell developed a massive body of work with his craft in such a profoundly focused manner that his progress became exponential. He was essentially able to work harder and longer than his peers. Though society saw this as a step back, his commitment propelled him forward.

In 2004, one year after graduating high school, Dorell was the 19th overall pick in the NBA draft, and he's now playing in his twelfth year in the NBA. The unshakable commitment to purpose and peak expression of self was such a powerful force that Dorell could be remarkably successful even after he didn't take the clear, intelligent choice and go for broke. It's clear that if Dorell continued on with baseball, his lack of desire and purpose in the pursuit would never have stood up against the ever-increasing challenges. In peak performance, talent is never enough. Dorell was undoubtedly gifted, but his unrelenting connection to going right enabled him to swim upstream against social pressures and all odds to find success in a place that looked irresponsible on paper. Whether the fork in the road is choosing an office job or playing a sport, the principles are the same. The highest expression of all of us, whatever that may be, is found within going right.

→ → →

For most of my life, going right meant seeking mastery in base-ball. Sports have an easily definable evaluative tool. In sports, you make the team, or you don't; you're safe, or you're out; you win, or you lose.

I not only knew that I wanted to be a Major League Baseball player, but that it would also take a herculean effort to get there. I would supplement hours of traditional team and individual train-ing with hundreds of swings in the backyard driving buckets and buckets of baseballs into a makeshift net. I knew deep down that my only chance at expressing my potential in this arena was to unearth it with my extensive body of work. I found a bottomless pit of potential for work capacity with my simple goal.

My mind raced with the information between every swing for insight and direction for adjustments for the next effort. I could find minute details with each repetition. Every swing was a leap-frog effort that compounded my experiences. I could see and recall the finest differences from swing to swing. This behavior would be priceless to any leader if they could bottle it and sell it to their followers. Imagine the quality of my work in the back yard applied to virtually any other task. The productivity and oppor-tunity for excellence is limitless.

You can't fake the desire to tap into this type of utility.

When I was fourteen, I got a hint of this dynamic. Even at that young age, I was something of a local prospect. I religiously tallied each game I played that year on an index card. I logged 171 games, nine more games than a full Major League season. I played for three teams simultaneously. For some time people joked that I was a "catcher for hire." I was in demand. One day a coach whom I didn't know called for a favor.

"Can you catch tonight? Game is at 7. Blair Field. There should be a good amount of scouts. We need a guy..."

I was much less skilled at saying no at age fourteen than I am now. I had the time to make it, and I didn't want to let this guy down. It was after 4:30PM. I remember vividly holding the phone and feeling an odd sense of weakness come over me. I usually operated with a layer of confidence that bordered on downright arrogance when it came to baseball.

I hastily began to get my gear and uniform together. As my dad drove us toward the Long Beach State campus, I realized why I felt so weird. I hadn't thought about that night's game at all. I had, until that moment, always mentally rehearsed, drilled, envisioned, and lived inside my future performances so that by the time the game came around, I had been there hundreds of times already. That night I ran out under the lights to join my temporary teammates for team stretch, and I felt naked and uncomfortable.

I suddenly felt like a novice without having that time to think through and mentally prepare for the evening. The difference was habitual high-level visualization practices. Years later in college and professional baseball, sports psychologists would come teach us a skill we learned to do automatically by pursuing something with a passion for excellence like going right. I felt at that moment that I was walking into a physics test without even opening the textbook.

If we look at our ability to create value as an open market with natural competition, value shows up because it stands out from the crowd. It doesn't pay to land in the middle of the bell curve. The notion that we ought to tackle everything in moderation is baseless. You'll notice that those who have success with moderation have simply earned a new normal where moderation is relative for them. We have to look for effective ways to create work structures that extend beyond normal to create value that positively impacts ourselves and our communities.

Every endeavor needs to have a powerful mindset to tackle what's ahead. How many days would John from my flight go to work with *that* type of rigorous mental presence and preparation to his tasks at hand? Going right enables allows us to prepare and develop greatness with deliberate practice.

CHAPTER 7

HOLD THE STANDARD

WE KNOW THAT going right is going to be a challenge. It requires that we evolve beyond our current means. Once we settle into the idea of a challenge, it becomes distinctly clear that best practices are beneficial. As a fitness professional, I see the ebb and flow of motivation wreak havoc on the goals and aspirations of countless men and women. Motivation is such a scarce resource and relying solely on it for any arduous undertaking is a recipe for disaster. Millions of Americans will start a fitness practice this year and quit shortly after. It's not altogether surprising. These individuals must show up to a giant facility where virtually no one knows (or cares) who they are or if they're there or not. Beyond the apathy, they then need to put themselves through challenging training. Most people are increasingly unsure as to what they should do or how they should do it. Training, even when you know what you're doing, is a long term commitment. Your body doesn't change quickly, the feedback loop is long and slow, and the work is hard. Of course, you can mitigate *some* of these pain points by hiring a personal trainer, but, at around $100 an hour, that's not always feasible.

A license plate sized piece of worn scrap wood, etched with the words "Motivated People Only," is securely fastened with wire to the rot iron gate it's posted on. This gate is the front of my gym, DEUCE Gym, and there is no place like it on Earth. Where Muscle Beach, the iconic outdoor training gym on the boardwalk in Venice Beach, is now an iconic tourist attraction without the life it once was, this place is thriving as a contemporary replacement.

Past the gate is an outdoor yard of patrons—all ages, sizes, and fitness levels—fronting an old auto service garage. The back wall looks menacing, as if it's stocked with weapons in a medieval movie. Chains, barbells, and a plethora of rigorous strength paraphernalia.

With half a dozen professional coaches, everyone is here to take part in something that demands personal excellence at every turn. It's a culture that often cracks the code on a life long pinball journey in and out of fad diets and fitness routines which leave most Americans short on results and long on frustration and waistlines.

Consider that this organization not only breeds the teachings of going right, the organization itself lives and breathes it. The motto at the facility is, "Hold the Standard," which begs the endless question, what are you becoming? From the top down, self-respect and personal evolution provide an overview for the organization. This culture begins to dole out going right principles for all involved. We practice commitment and deep practice. We're teaching the 'how' and the 'why' rather than just telling them the 'what' that will produce the most sweat.

Adversity is a daily, unavoidable element of our culture. The training is not easy, and it never will be. This, in many ways, is a dose of adversity that inoculates our students. With exposure, they become resilient. They learn to face these struggles head-on. And they learn how to focus, to be in the moment for highly skilled, high-intensity training. Our athletes are forever matched challenge-wise with a relative skill set or experience level. This triangulates for a perfect stretch goal scenario that is ripe for peak human expression. And there are a host of unavoidable highly transferable skills made available to someone enrolled in challenging physical and mental training that provides tangible utility in relationships and at work. The result of this environment is a scenario where more is possible with the group than could ever be possible on an individual basis.

By the time most people get to DEUCE, however, they've started and stopped a handful of different training practices. What they don't know when they get there, though, is that this is the end of the road for them. Likely for the first time in their lives, they will be able to be compliant to a movement practice, work hard, and take control of their physical and mental fitness. How do they do it?

These people are held accountable, supported, and insulated by a community. A community of support is vital for going right and can be incredibly influential. It's so important that we explain the exact dynamic to prospective students at my gym. Coming to DEUCE is like being dropped in the middle of a river. Just by being here, surrounded by the community, people will begin to make progress. The current is going to provide momentum. If the member is willing to do some swimming, then watch out, because then they'll really get moving. Community is key, and as human beings, we do a great job of adapting to our environment.

It's in our DNA to seek risk avoidance and succumb to the path of least resistance. That's how we got here in the first place. We're evolutionarily tugged toward the safest and easiest route. In a community that supports your peak expression, the path is easier! When I'm outside of my intentionally designed bubble of work-out obsessed friends, behavior becomes at odds with my surroundings. People give me defensive looks and try to calm their nerves by making flexing mannerisms with nervous laughter. In my world, squatting, flipping tires, and dragging sleds aren't just normal, my community wouldn't accept it if I slacked in my level of activity. In many ways, my community is like insurance from failure.

→ → →

If you have any experience with high performing teams, you know that there is an invisible force that drives group performance beyond the sum of its parts. Many of the best teams, from NBA courts, business boardrooms, and the battalions on the battlefield, perform at the highest level because they are aligned on decision making that mimics the going right process. There is a distinct connection to uncompromising commitment, deep practice, resistance to adversity, propensity to flow states, and the development of highly transferable skills. In a military context, we recognize our special forces as masters of what's called a force multiplier. This is a mechanism that allows for exponential growth in output with the same amount of effort.

Going right is an action of progress. Consider a factory that mass produces hats. With two dozen workers at various stations, it can become monotonous. Brims are made like the brims are made. The crowns are shaped like the crowns and so on. If management observes that one worker can produce their share of fifteen hats per day, this will become the socialized expectation. The utility of workflow is equal to the utility of what one worker could produce (15 hats) times twenty-four. Add a worker, and you've now increased the force of the factory by one. This growth is linear.

We have Henry Ford to thank for this kind of scalability, but we ought to be grateful that we didn't stop there in our development. This example of organizational growth is quite archaic. The numbers may seem to appear a matter of fact, but there's more juice to be squeezed here. Consider that the somewhat arbitrary force number of fifteen hats per day becomes a socialized expectation where producing fourteen hats would be a failure. Sixteen would be an overachievement that would go unrewarded and possibly frowned upon by colleagues keen on holding to the norm. This quota diminishes community culture and creates a ceiling on the team's potential. Are fifteen imperfect hats better than fourteen perfect ones? Where production improves, efficiency develops naturally, and the factory workers are capable of making a sixteenth or seventeenth hat of the same or better quality but are compelled to follow socialized directions rather than innovate. Again, the utility of the team remains one equals one.

Purpose changes everything. Sure, there are times when brims and crowns are made to follow some sort of direction. But there is a force multiplier when an organization is enrolled in an evolutionary purpose. Workers are compelled to fulfill intrinsic standards as well as externally imposed expectations, where they answer to the spirit of the mission, not a quota. Making the sixteenth hat with quality is rewarded in going right. As is only making fourteen, because extra care was needed. In a team that adheres to this approach, best practices naturally emerge because no artificial norms are impeding what's best for the team. Members can, and will, over-achieve. Adding a team member to an organization isn't a 1X addition. High-performance teams can 10X their force production with an MVP player. This is the future of organizations.

Staying true to the principle that says we must transcend and include our evolutionary stages, going right has the same application with teams and small groups. Teams that have enough structure to share a common goal also benefit from having a stronger expression of commitment, deeper practice work habits, more resilience to adversity, flow, transferable skills, and even increased complexity.

It is vital that the leadership of an organization understands and helps to foster a going right mentality. When members of the team are embracing the going right approach, it has positive effects developmentally on those inside of the organization. Observations that challenge our assumptions break our developmental frame.

→ → →

In 2007, while at the University of San Diego, things really came to a boiling point in our locker room. There were plenty of ways we kept a tight ship in our organization. As teammates, we were unfailingly direct. Communication was clear, and the standards were high. The team didn't rely on coaches and adults to direct us, we self-policed, all with a shared purpose. In many ways, the team was a living, breathing, self-sustaining organism that used collective energy to grow.

We were a diverse group of individuals—morons, genius minds, athletic freaks of nature, and talentless grinders—committed to a clear purpose. Not only was decentralized leadership possible, but there was also exponential potential for work capacity and quality. The unifying power of the team's commitment to going right allowed for freedom we rarely see in low-performance groups. Everyone was ready to lead, and everyone was ready to follow. The organization, then, could move and adapt to the stimulus placed upon it in real time. This is the same language used to describe Navy SEAL teams. After all, you can't raid a compound only to discover there are more insurgents than expected and tiptoe back out to ask your boss what you should do next. Teams can't possibly excel if they need to call timeout every time they're faced with adversity.

When issues arose on the team, they were policed and handled by the team. No coaches had to sort the issue out. The culture sorted it out. In low-performance organizations, disputes are typically resolved (largely ineffectively and unsustainably) from the top down. Naturally, these organic regulatory systems take less top-down energy and are received more genuinely. In an organization working toward the going right approach, feedback is an authentic language that keeps the group on the rails and working toward the goal. Furthermore, feedback is exchanged in all directions, regardless of titles. The highest performers operating closest to their highest potential lust for negative feedback because they know it is the source of how they can level up.

Chef Antonia Lofaso, the celebrity chef, and owner of Black Market Liquor Bar, Scopa Italian Roots, and DAMA three of the top restaurants in Los Angeles, is always hungry for feedback. Antonia is a gregarious and forceful presence in her restaurants. I try to eat at her restaurants as often as possible. On a recent spring evening, she came out of the kitchen to say hello and eagerly asked me, "How is everything? Tell me. Don't hold back."

While I should have known better, I sputtered a quick compliment. "Everything is great, chef," I said. "As always, thank you."

She glared at me for a moment and then shot back, "Oh stop it! Give me something."

"Ok, ok," I said. Something was a little different in that day's seafood salad.

"Ugh! Thank you! Thank you!" she exclaimed. "I've been dealing with this onion ordeal in the crudo bar." She was legitimately grateful to hear some criticism.

Antonia has been classically trained in French cooking. After attending The French Culinary Institute in New York, she paid her dues again and again. Much of these dues were paid under award-winning, world renown chef, Wolfgang Puck. Antonia not only transcended this rite of passage to be a chef, but she's also found success as a viable business owner and tv personality. Not only does her food speaks for itself, but her character also bleeds out of the kitchen and into the households of millions of viewers on shows like *Top Chef, Cutthroat Kitchen*, and *Restaurant Startup*. Yet, when you eat her food, she doesn't want to know what you liked about it. She wants *negative* feedback.

There is a theme here among the world's highest performers. The science behind Antonia's desire to hear about her shortcomings is strategic. It's not that she's tired of hearing praise. She likes a compliment as much as the next chef, but when it comes to her craft, she can't do much with a compliment. Criticism, however, is useful information that she can act upon. If you've spent any time managing people and reading basic texts on communication such as "How to Win Friends and Influence People," you know that people want to be right and are far more motivated by positive reinforcement. So what gives?

High performers recognize the power of negative feedback. Performance trumps feeling good at the elite level. While it *feels* better to hear that the steak tartare was perfection, this doesn't help to gain a competitive advantage. Hearing that the seafood salad is heavy on onions, however, has within it a clue to improvement, and the subsequent performance gains it can provide.

→ → →

In a range of leadership and organizational studies, the rigors of organizational goals, especially in business, are tethered more to performance than to emotional fulfillment needs. An organization using a going right approach must yield results, regardless of how good it does or doesn't feel. Going right affords organizations to latch onto a deep-rooted, purposeful commitment. These organizations are then able to create a large work capacity as well as the ability to execute deliberate practice. Their commitment to purpose also makes them more resilient to opposing adverse forces.

Yvon Chouinard, the founder of Patagonia, said in his memoir "Let My People Go Surfing," "When I die and go to hell, the devil is going to make me the marketing director for a cola company. I'll be in charge of trying to sell a product that no one needs, is identical to is competition, and can't be sold on its merits." Chouinard, who has created a multi-national brand with hundreds of millions of dollars in revenue, did so without ever losing sight of his or the business's evolutionary purpose. Patagonia is often the source of scholarly insights into organizational culture and leadership.

Some of the most advanced organizational structures are called Evolutionary Teal Organizations, a concept introduced by Frederic Laloux, a former McKinsey consultant introduced in his book, "Reinventing Organizations." Laloux uses a color-coded system for organizational advancement that mimics conscious development. In this system teal is the highest level and Patagonia is one of the few large companies to have achieved this level.

Teal organizations enjoy peak expression through unique characteristics. Distributed decision making, for example, is vital. Top down, hierarchical management is archaic, lacks agility, and hardly empowers members of the organization. Effective teams are built with members that are, as they say in the SEAL teams, "Ready to lead and ready to follow." The parallels between the SEALs and Patagonia are not far-fetched. Subscribing to leadership values that force decision making up the chain of command underachieves on the battlefield and in retail. As much as it's ineffective to ask the platoon chief for permission to shoot, Teal organizations empower all team members to have their finger on the trigger at work. General responsibility and accountability is increased across the group but so is the opportunity to contribute and evolve. If your every move is approved, dictated, or instructed, what then are you accountable to?

Purpose is critical in any endeavor. Purpose, in Teal organizations such as Patagonia, is a living, breathing, and evolving concept. These organizations are held to rigorous standards and best practices to produce excellent goods and services with an underlying sense of purpose. This purpose, like the roles of its members, can and should evolve over time. Patagonia in its infancy is distinctly different from the massive corporation is it today. There are surely themes and values that are consistent, but the conditions and environments have changed and will continue to change. Organizations get stuck when they cannot evolve.

Business school students are often taught about how the railroad industry failed to evolve. Assuming they were in the business of trains, they were eventually bested by other companies (such as airlines) who better understood that they were not in the business of trains, but *travel*. The consumer, after all, isn't looking for a train ride. They are looking to change their location. Railroad tycoons in the early part of the 20th century were insulated and on top of the world. Their lack of evolutionary purpose and subsequent lack of agility confirmed their slow death in the travel business.

There is particular freedom that comes when a business is held to a higher standard of excellence beyond the bottom line. It starts to build a world where others don't need to lose for you to win. Patagonia competes against itself to an increasingly rigorous and complex standard for their own excellence. In the process of doing so, they've innovated the production of not just outdoor gear, but the entire set of possibilities for the sourcing, manufacturing, and repair of apparel goods. They did so to stay true to a guiding purpose. You can start to understand why Chouinard's hell involves working for a cola company.

We talk regularly at DEUCE Gym about striving to exist as an Evolutionary Teal Organization. We often described our structure as the most sustainable form of leadership. While it's possible to have a remarkably successful organization by most measures with a much less evolved organizational structure, we find that the Teal organization has the most fruitful return for everyone involved. Consider an organization with a strong product and exceptional leadership. Such an organization is still pushed along with the oversight, policing, and motivational drive of the leader. Contrast that approach with a Teal organization where everyone is held to standards to produce and evolve. The responsibility and accountability is just as strong at the bottom as it is at the top. In fact, there is no top or bottom. There is no scapegoat to blame above or below you. There's just a group intrinsically motivated to achieve its own greatness.

CHAPTER 8

CURIOSITY IS THE SEED

CURIOSITY IS THE seed for commitment. Nurturing curiosity creates an opportunity to harvest our lives' richest commitments.

When we find purpose, fulfillment, and challenge in something, our desire tends to last longer. It's these desires that stick and which can take on the characteristics of what it means to embrace going right. We're always making choices in our lives—from what's for dinner to who to see on Saturday night—but it's the meaningful choices that have lasting power. I don't play professional baseball anymore, but I still find interests and activities that give me more fulfillment and demand a higher expression of myself.

One place I seek this fulfillment and where I can see this peak expression in action around me is at the home of Gabrielle Reece and surfing legend Laird Hamilton. Gabby and Laird have created a formalized training regimen called XPT. This system, which has online resources and destination retreats, was born in their backyard from their own work-outs, not just of their hard-charging achievement lifestyle, but out of curiosity.

On any given day at Gabby and Laird's house, up a winding canyon road in the Malibu hills, there are several dozen people taking part in one of the more unique fitness courses around. The training day is a loose journey through pool exercises—replete with goggles and dumbbells (and an ability to stay calm underwater), saunas, and ice-baths. Each takes a level of faith and curiosity to complete.

I've tried the ice bath a handful of times, and it gets a little easier each time. The first time I whined and thrashed silently with a terrible grimace and quiet moan. Lately, I can stand about three minutes with a marginally better attitude. I try to get in the tub a couple times a week, and I'm still amazed at the cold. I've competed in the North American Strongman nationals—lifting giant atlas stones and deadlifting car axles—and yet my pain threshold in a tub of ice is near nil. But my curiosity continues to drive me forward.

As XPT has grown beyond the comfy confines of Gabby and Laird's backyard pool and into the gyms and homes of a larger, more disparate group, I've had the opportunity to speak at one of the experiences. My most important message wasn't of how to adequately lift an impossibly heavy object, it was about curiosity. Individuals who are tapping into their deepest potential, participating in fulfilling relationships, enriching their highest-expression lifestyles, are people who embrace curiosity. This curiosity is, after all, the fire for our pursuits.

→ → →

I'm always looking for next-level experiences to throw myself into. Recently I've decided to dedicate time to learning jiu-jitsu. Jiu-Jitsu is an incredibly intense and violent sport. It is not something to undertake without full focus, determination, and conviction (unless you don't mind coming away battered, bruised, and injured). Emotional motivators help but are rarely enough to create long-lasting, remarkable experiences and results.

In my jiu-jitsu gym, Street Sports Brazilian Jiu-Jitsu in Santa Monica, the mats are old and worn, and the walls are covered in dated photos with a certain patina and vintage pride reminiscent of an old weightlifting gym. Street Sports is a haven for black belts. Most of the students in my 7AM class are many years into their practice, while I barely know how to tie my belt. I am a lowly white belt, the bottom of a many runged ladder of respectability in the sport.

There's an apocryphal story about the belt system that describes how white belts, after years of hard work and fighting, became worn and dirty. The black belt was a recognition of a belt blackened by experience. There's a certain honesty to the story. That's how progression works, after all. You can't skip steps. It's in the actual experience of transcending one status to advance to the next that we build on the preceding foundation. A person has to learn, have success, fail, and eventually transcend being a beginner before they can become an intermediate.

With difficult endeavors, it can be tough to sustain interest, and the emotional drivers that get someone involved often aren't enough to keep people coming back. The pursuits that speak to us most deeply are the ones that give us nourishing fulfillment, the ones we find purpose in, and the ones that ask for the best in us.

Jiu-jitsu is new in my world, but it's satisfies these deeper calling questions. It satisfies my curiosity, something I can't imagine the highest expression of myself without. When we take a going right approach we are tapping into what is most uniquely ourselves. The struggle in the early days of a jiu-jitsu practice is just like the struggle of any new practice. There is a lot to learn and life as a beginner is filled with failure. As with any new endeavor, the initial steps are not very intuitive. When learning a new skill, however, we have a deeper connection if we are using the skills from a going right approach.

Decision making continues to evolve for all of us. I intend to dig into what types of decision making initiates people beginning journeys. What drives curiosity before idle interest? I want to know what kinds of decision making yields the best results. And how going right plays into those decisions. Who's happier? Who's more committed? Who's able to put in more work? Does one do more *effective* work? Who is better equipped to weather the storm?

→ → →

Curiosity has always been a key driver of human culture and advancement. Yuval Noah Harari, the Israeli historian, and philosopher mentioned in chapter three has written about consciousness, free will and intelligence in his books "Sapiens" and "Homo Deus," and specifically about how curiosity is the single point of differentiation between a culture being an evolutionary winner or not. It was the determining factor in whether empires rose and fell.

Curiosity begins with an important presumption: that we don't know. Hariri posits that there was a cognitive revolution about 50,000 years ago—when humans rose above the neanderthals—punctuated by the birth of science. This transition brought about a shift in consciousness globally, from a mythological belief in explaining the world to a scientific one.

In "Sapiens" Harari highlights later stages of curiosity. When Europe began colonizing other continents, their ships weren't just loaded with guns, they also sent scientists. Even with India and China accounting for 80% of the world economy in the 18th century, Europe became the center of the global sphere of power by advancing their world view. Curiosity has shaped our world as we know it.

→ → →

Curiosity can be the initial spark required for any new pursuit, but it also continues to pay dividends if we're aware of it and foster it in our lives. The abundance of curiosity embodied in Laird and Gabby, and all of their endeavors and pursuits is almost un-paralleled. These are two highly successful people who do not rest on their laurels. It's a constant evolution for them.

I remember being floored with inspiration sitting in the sauna hearing Laird talk about his upcoming winter surfing and sailing in Hawaii. Someone asked, "Are you looking forward to getting back out there? I mean, do you find it hard to keep going or do you just love it that much?"

"I'm completely fired up," he said, "because with all the hy-drofoil stuff we're doing and the fine tuning that's going on, we went faster this year than we did last year and I know we're going to go out there and do things next year that we couldn't do this year."

Laird is considered the most legendary big-wave surfer of all-time. He's done everything but still manages to be the most curi-ous person in the room. The engineers that develop the world-class racing boats for America's Cup Champion, Oracle USA, work with Laird to tinker, question old designs, and develop new frontiers in mastering the water. These types of practices and, most definitely, these types of results don't come from a mindset that thinks it knows it all. For a guy who's earned the right to say he knows a thing or two, Laird chooses to forgo this certainty for the beautiful uncertainty of curiosity.

→ → →

Curiosity doesn't only provide the groundwork for new discoveries. It is the underpinning of commitment. Human evolution is a little two-sided. The natural inkling to seek safety is countered by our evolutionary connection with curiosity. Our general sense for wonder is the fuel for exploration. Our natural curiosity led us out of mysticism and into the advent of the sciences. Nature rewards survival, yet dominance in the developing world rested on those who set sail into unknown horizons. In critical periods of human history it was the curious who prevailed. The polarity between our natural drive for risk avoidance and curiosity is at the heart of going right. Watering the seeds of curiosity is the most important step in developing true commitment. And commitment is the first component in going right.

Commitment is our willingness to continue forward regardless of time and circumstances. It's generally rare because it requires enduring hardship. Commitment requires an opt-in for more heartache, more struggle, or more work. True commitment is rare in most people but let's examine how it maintains its value.

To understand the true value of commitment, we'll need to note a simple observation about the world we live in. There is but one certainty in life for all people: uncertainty. The future is dictated by forces and outcomes out of our control. Because we all are at risk of quitting, commitment is one of the most valuable characteristics people can develop. Quitting is a contagion. It eliminates the opportunity for mastery and its residual value. If we teach ourselves to opt for paths of least resistance, we will find it easier and easier to succumb to these paths.

When looking at a series of decisions, developing a strong practice of commitment can be used as a base to battle the oncoming adversities. Without the hard-earned skill of commitment, a human being becomes a reactionary being, molded by their environment. This robs humanity of its freedom to choose. Lacking commitment in all we do creates disturbing effects in our lives. Lacking control over our environment is the seed for depression and victimization. The ability to learn, practice, and develop deep-rooted commitment makes a foundational case for greater personal value while being absolutely critical to the expression of human happiness.

The less likely you are to quit something, the more likely people are to find the right pursuit and purpose. With a purpose, we can endure in unimaginable ways. Consider the commitment of a parent to a child. Children often provide a paradigm shift giving new parents a new meaning. When a parent identifies with a new purpose as a parent, they commit to an entire life of love and service to their child. There are few other relationships as one-sided as a parent. Parents give up sleep, time, even their life savings for their commitment to that child.

As humans, we have an underlying common admiration for the idea of resilience. We *love* when folks tough it out and do remarkable things. We write songs, create motion pictures, and share stories of men and women in scenarios that are ripe for quitting, yet choose to endure anyway. This attraction is in our DNA. Conversely, we're all quitters if we're doing the wrong things, especially when we're enrolled in things without a clear purpose.

The simple truth is that when you're in the wrong place, with the wrong people, working for the wrong reasons, quitting isn't just a thought. Quitting is an inevitable reality. These environments dismiss our potential, erode our level of fulfillment, and undermine our ability to provide greatness.

This alone is a cause for notice. We are the most robust versions of ourselves when we're chasing purpose. Purpose enables us to know commitment honestly. Conversely, jobs and relationships which don't embody purpose make people fragile and weak and prone to quitting. The irony is that this perceived safety net makes people less likely to succeed. It's a story we've seen play out time and time again. It's sometimes difficult to find examples of people that don't burn out of a lifestyle that is outside of their passion and purpose.

However, when you're living your dream—a life filled with purpose and passion—the struggles and despair fade away. When extra work comes across someone's desk, with purpose, it is not a burden but a part of moving forward. Shop owners gladly turn in ninety-hour workweeks to water the fruits of their labor. An athlete with dreams of a college scholarship will gladly come early and stay late. True commitment continues to yield more upside when it comes to objective advantages like work capacity, tenacity, and durability.

Want to learn commitment? Nurture your curiosities with reckless abandon.

CHAPTER 9

COMMITMENT

IN THE MIDDLE of an urban, sun-drenched park in Santa Fe, New Mexico, two men, Tait Fletcher, and Arlan Sanford, are swinging thirty-two-inch sticks at each other, circling with an eye toward an opening to attack. They're wearing masks and gloves, but that's it for protective gear, and the sound of rattan on flesh is sharp and resonant.

Sanford, who runs a martial arts fight group called The Dog Brothers, has created a training program and fight series that resembles an unsanctioned Fight Club. When fighters break through an opponent's sticks, then knees, elbows, and fists start flying until one fighter submits. It's a brutal, often bloody, no rules public spectacle which requires the most serious commitment.

A circle surrounds the fight. A group of mostly men, watching intently as the battle rages. Nobody is stepping in to break it up. There is little reaction other than acknowledgment for a   clean strike as the men tumble to the floor. It's violent and fast.

Tait is every bit of his 6' 3" frame; and a menacing 240 pounds, covered in tattoos. He has soft green eyes that belie the battered and bruised face. He's bald with an aggressive beard with three long braids that hang down in front of his neck. Tait has a calm, soothing presence but his ability to inflict pain and damage is severe. This public park fight club drew Tait in a way most people would find confounding. It paved the way for a life-long pursuit of mastery in combat.

Stick fighting took Tait on a decade-long ride to the Ultimate Fighting Championships. It was a spark of curiosity that fed a thirst in Tait, which in turn led to an irreplaceable commitment. "I distinctly remember finishing a fight," Tait told me over a feast at a mutual friend's restaurant. As a layman, I sat swirling wine in my glass trying to place myself in his shoes. What seemed like a terrifying game of 'who's the better killer' apparently had the space for peace and reflection for Tait. The highly trained fighter had a competency in that environment that allowed him to see and experience more than I could when faced in the same situa-tion. "I was thinking nothing but thoughts of gratitude," Tait ex-plained. "Here we are, two men inflicting real violence on each other and all I had was sheer gratitude for the moment."

With bloody sticks whizzing past Tait's head, the environment was so rich for learning, development, and a deep understanding about responsiveness and responsibility that it created a sensory experience where time slowed and epinephrine and dopamine flooded the brain. This was a marriage to the moment for Tait. When these men squared off in combat, the circumstances presented a perfect environment to learn about oneself. It was an endless challenge. After all, the consequences were steep. These stakes, like ultra-accountability, rewards positive adaptation and extreme honest feedback loops.

Tait's curiosity was a seed for his commitment. The Swedish psychologist K. Anders Ericsson talks, in his book "Peak: Secrets from the New Science of Expertise," about how curiosity leads to commitment and it usually starts with play. We fall in love with what is fun. "This desire," Ericsson writes, "to play serves as a child's initial motivation to try out one thing or another, to see what is interesting and what is not, and to engage in various activities that will help them build their skills. At this point they're developing simple skills, of course—arranging chess pieces on a chessboard, throwing a ball, swinging a racket, organizing marbles by shape or pattern—but for future experts, this playful interaction with whatever has caught their interest is their first step toward what will eventually become their passion." Tait's backyard passion led to an intrinsically motivated commitment that took his life on a remarkably rewarding ride.

Tait moved from stick fighting in parks to jiu-jitsu where he quickly rose through the ranks and, ultimately, became a world champion black belt with successful performances at international events such as the Mundials and the Pan Ams. He then moved on to mixed martial arts where he was plucked out to be in a new reality show, *Ultimate Fighter,* produced by the UFC to develop characters for its growing fan base.

Tait has since successfully transcended his fighting career to being a serial entrepreneur and an actor. But the devil *isn't* in the details. Tait's process and progression are a classic study of going right. To endure such a rite of passage, there must be a commitment to a long road-type pursuit. The journey does all the work providing adversity, introspection, challenge, and insight into who we really are.

As Tait tells it, he and his fellow UFC fighters, including superstars like Keith "The Dean of Mean" Jardine, fought because they loved it. Tait didn't get into fighting for the glamour and fame. When he began, there was no money in the sport, no name in lights, no octagon. This is not to say that wanting fame and fortune is wrong or dishonorable. Attempting to succeed based solely on that external reward, however, is rarely enough of a qualifying force. For Tait and his era of fighters, any notoriety, fame, or fortune was merely accidental.

Tait's commitment grew out of intrinsic reasons that made him feel positive and rewarded and challenged his current state. He committed to self-discovery. His quest to master fighting came with punishing accountability and feedback. This same feedback loop in training and in competition forces the athlete to challenge their assumptions.

Fighting was an opportunity for Tait to drive his own personal evolution. The result was a remarkable understanding of commitment. Even if you dropped a Tait clone into the world to follow in his footsteps— same gyms, coaches, sparring partners—without the same commitment it's a life that wouldn't be replicated. There is an intangible advantage to Tait's pursuit. His deep commitment is a more authentically accurate portrayer of himself.

→ → →

It would be difficult to debate whether there is a more consistently performing military organization than the US Navy SEAL Teams. The Navy cannot invest in and risk human lives by putting people through the SEAL training unless they are fully committed to the idea. It would otherwise cost American lives.

The hard truth is that people that would rather do something else with their life cannot possibly be as effective as people who find satisfaction in what they're doing. That's the utility of commitment. Just as there is no substitute for a person's potential when going right. Recognizing and taking part in unshakable commitment is the first attribute of going right. Training to become a Navy SEAL is notoriously grueling. The attrition rate is close to 80%. Basic Underwater Demolition/SEAL training (BUD/S) is the most significant training step in completing the training. It's in BUD/S that these candidates are molded from hopeful, talented, motivated individuals into teams of disciplined soldiers that would rather die than quit. The six-month process is paved with discomfort. Nearly every move these soldiers make is under scrutiny, and the SEAL instructors use adversity to test the ranks.

BUD/S is a physical juggernaut, but it pales in comparison to the mental warfare these young sailors endure. During the infamous "hell week" sailors will get roughly four or five hours of sleep in total. Throughout the training process, the sailors are consistently reminded that they can quit at any time. When they do—also referred to as "ringing out"—the recruit rings a brass bell and places his numbered helmet on the ground in front of all the remaining sailors. Quitters aren't alone in this program, and the attrition rate is a point of pride for the teams.

What can we take from these observations? There's minimal possibility that someone can contribute to the highest level task if they're also harboring a desire to quit. Commitment pays. Commitment is paramount with the highest expression of self, and it's with commitment that we begin to examine the indicators of going right.

→ → →

Thank God Dave Grohl doesn't work at the bank. Every time I find myself talking to a bank teller behind the glass—organizing that little deposit slip for me—I often wonder what a waste it would be for someone as committed as Dave Grohl is to music to find himself carefully copying down my bank account number. These are the things I think about. I don't think about it because I'm generally demeaning of people that work in banking, or because I think Dave Grohl is a different *kind* of human. But there aren't enough hours in the day for Dave Grohl to contribute to banking what he can with music. There isn't a motivating salary large enough to force love and commitment to the duties of bank teller that Dave Grohl has for music.

The utility in passionate commitment, like Dave Grohl's love for music, is the necessary start to guiding our highest value decision making. If we're looking for how we can be most useful, we ought to be looking for what we can be most committed to. This process of curiosity, discovery, and subsequent commitment is the richest source of human expression.

If anyone is making a choice to avoid risk while forgoing their true goals, then they are going to be less effective in life. Imagine Jean-Michel Basquiat in human resources. Or Beethoven in the patent office. Mrs. Weems, my first-grade teacher in Santa Monica, California, fits the mold as well. Teaching was her passion and the perfect expression of her potential. She was a remarkable teacher and thank god she didn't pursue acting. Her decision to take the going right approach with her career taught her commitment that propped up a forty-year-long career which benefited countless kids. Like me.

In each of the examples mentioned above, the subjects' paths were of the highest utility to themselves and those around them, *and* it was a more challenging choice than the alternative. Deciding to pursue greatness in music or art or teaching isn't for the weary and success if it comes, is only a by-product.

Is including an example like Grohl's unfair? How much does luck and pure talent come into play? Grohl wasn't lucky once or even twice. Nirvana wasn't a lottery ticket. In its early days, the band had incredible turnover and worked diligently to get the right members. The Foo Fighters were never a foregone conclusion. Their first album was recorded in individual segments, each recorded and performed by Grohl himself. After shopping his demo around the industry, Capitol Records signed Grohl, who suddenly had a record deal, but no band.

Success didn't merely happen to Grohl. He created his own victory.

The commitment to Grohl's career was the result of a thirty-year-long endeavor. Even if you believe in love at first sight, not only surviving but thriving beyond the initial meeting into a lifetime of love takes time, effort, complex levels of understanding. The same is true for an outlandish desire to be a rockstar, which begins with genuine curiosity and attraction. Dave Grohl had humble beginnings. In 2004, Grohl told *Modern Drummer* magazine that "I had a chair that was next to my bed, and I would kneel down on the floor and put a pillow between my legs to use as my snare. I would use the chair to my left as a hi-hat and use the bed as toms and cymbals. And I would play to these records until there was condensation dripping from the windows."

When Grohl was young, he worked in a furniture warehouse and played music as often as he could. It wasn't good music. Grohl maintains he wasn't naturally good at drumming, nor did he know many guitar chords. He just knew that to be a successful musician he'd have to blow people away. So he tackled a task he had so much passion for that he could never quit it. He took the going right approach. Decades later, he stayed committed long enough to have fifteen Grammy's to show for it.

For us mere mortals, we don't need to bang against our furniture until sweat fogs up our bedroom. But we can easily compare and contrast levels of passion. Expecting extraordinary outcomes from oneself without a deep commitment is misguided. Grohl plugged into and nurtured a commitment that didn't come with future certainty of success.

Yes, Grohl has a level of innate talent. The value one brings to a craft is precisely one of the strong logical reasons for going right. Dave Grohl is a surefire candidate for the most talented guy on his block. His genuine love for music tethered him to a commitment strong enough to delve into a life-long pursuit of earning that talent.

It's commitment that produces *these* results. And it's these results that speak for themselves. In "This is a Call," a biography of Grohl by Paul Brannigan, Grohl recounts a concert where he "had a profound revelation as I was staring at my mother and my sister on the side of the stage: that I wrote a song on the back of a fucking AM/PM receipt, and now 60,000 people are singing it. I honestly felt like the luckiest guy in the world." It's the commitment of a young drummer from Warren, Ohio that was a result of *his* passion. To learn commitment, and uncover what's possible when you pursue your highest self.

The difference between a person acting towards their ultimate purpose and another who isn't is stark. We could place another, less committed person on Dave Grohl's journey and end up with the opposite result. In instances where the conditions became difficult Grohl (as we now know) would continue where most would quit.

It's completely normal to be fearful of pursuing one's wildest dreams. This fear is often the reason there is a crossroads in our lives as we navigate our dreams and our safety net. Every Navy SEAL I have ever met (and there have been quite a few) has a habit of slipping in this SEAL adage: "Suffer the pain of discipline or suffer the pain of regret." Regret, of course, lasts forever. Ask any heartbroken man or woman who talks about the one that got away.

→ → →

The idea of commitment is painfully real for anyone who's set out on the challenging path to pursue going right. There are, after all, seemingly higher stakes when taking this approach. It can quickly feel as though we're taking on risk and danger. We feel like there's more to lose when we are in a perfect relationship, our dream job, or our ideal lifestyle.

Imagine the poor recruits going into Navy SEAL training. They're surrounded by high-performance individuals who, seemingly, are all remarkable candidates. Yet, in all likelihood, the people on either side of them won't be there in the end. Or maybe they are the ones who won't make the cut. When we believe this choice is our purpose, the fear of failure can become overwhelming. Embarking on this kind of endeavor can feel scary, and a strong commitment is required to take on greater and greater challenges. If it didn't, we'd just quit when things got hard. Luckily for those taking the going right approach, the depth of our commitment can be met with increasingly challenging environments. And we can endure more under an increasingly challenging set of circumstances. Commitment facilitates survival in challenging environments. Challenging environments facilitate excellence.

The high value of commitment is as useful when building the world's finest warriors as it is in becoming a proficient business leader. In fact, if a person is unable to quit—regardless of the difficulty or the challenge presented—then they're likely on the right track.

CHAPTER 10

GOOD, BETTER, BEST

THE DEL REY American Little League (DRALL) field was far from epic. The field was maintained by our dads, a collection of middle-aged white-collar guys helping their sons out. They juggled various agrarian titles like director of field operations or some other over formalized volunteer job title for the three month season. They'd edge the grass around the infield cutout as best they could with a shed full of used tools and a tractor that lasted my entire childhood. I can still smell the gasoline stench that filled the equipment shed. Or my dad's favorite trick after a rare rainfall: pour some gas on the infield dirt and ignite the wet areas to burn off some of the moisture.

One year, as an alert and eager ten-year-old, I remember suddenly being awestruck while sitting with my teammates on the field. Three towering men entered the field via the outfield fence dressed in *real* Major League uniforms. It was like real life "Field of Dreams." The uniforms were immaculate. The rough cut grass and the thought of my dad tending the field with flammable gas can didn't match the majestic white uniforms walking our way. A group of noisy seagulls chirped away providing an odd soundtrack for our guests. I thought of myself as a big shot then. It was my first year in the "majors," and I was the first pick in the draft. In my head this meant I was a team leader, was primed to take the team to the postseason and, most importantly, I was on track for my future Major League goals. Adolescent disillusionment goes unchecked in a lot of areas.

Our field was known as the "big field" with fences that were two hundred feet from home plate. But as the three figures walked across it, I suddenly realized the *entire* field would fit in the infield of a Major League ballpark. The home runs we talked about with the lore of Greek mythology were infield pop outs to the gentlemen walking our way. My teammates and I may have been young, but we were all physically gifted boys who imagined we would one day play professional ball. David Ohger, kneeling to my right, hit home runs that kids talked about for years. Todd Smith, sitting cross-legged in front of me, came from a family of freak athletes who all played Division I athletics. He threw so hard he scared people half to death when they stepped into the batter's box. Quinten Daniels, fumbling around with a ball in his glove behind me, went on to play free safety for the University of Washington. We all were dreamers, and today we'd get to learn from real pros.

When these ghost-like guests made their way to the twenty-five ballplayers, there wasn't a peep from the group. These were real baseball players, and that's all the mattered. Reggie and Tye Waller were brothers who both spent time in the Major Leagues. Tye was then the first base coach for the Oakland A's, and Reggie was a sports agent. With them was Mike Davis, wearing his own Los Angeles Dodgers uniform. For the day they would be our coaches in a makeshift clinic.

We spent the time running drills, getting hands-on coaching, and focusing on fundamentals of the game. For a few hours at least we all felt like Major Leaguers. It's one thing to dismiss your father's advice but when a pro player tells you to catch "with two hands," it suddenly becomes the best way to catch. It was during this makeshift camp on our little unassuming baseball field that I was suddenly struck by the power of coaching and mentorship. I was tremendously affected by their presence and their words.

"Good, better, best. Never let it rest," demanded Davis in his crisp white Dodger uniform. "Until the good becomes the better and the better becomes the best." His words did an effective job of illustrating progression, an unrelenting work ethic, and a clear path to big goals. It emphasized process. It glamorized the pursuit. It was a road map as clear as day for me, and I wrote it in permanent marker on the inside brim of my hat. And then on every hat for every team I went on to play for.

What's interesting about this pep talk is that while it was compelling and motivating to my teammates and to me, these emotions aren't enough to drive any person further along the path to their dreams. Consider the audience for this pep talk. We were a couple of dozen young baseball players who were unanimously enthralled with the sport. We were the best players and the most motivated players. Mike, Reggie, and Tye had us rapt, and when they said "you *can* accomplish your crazy goals" and "you *are* good enough to get a scholarship and one day wear a uniform like mine," it's incredibly motivating. I had chills hearing at the time. It's literally an emotional appeal to chase a common goal.

This type of emotional appeal is moving. And it can be particularly empowering. Our emotions are powerful drivers. For all the young players sitting in the audience that day listening to Davis tell us to follow our dreams "until the better becomes the best," it was motivation to charge into the future.

Motivation, however, is finicky. Often motivation can mobilize us, but it rarely sustains us. At some point motivation dries up; we stop thinking with our hearts and start analyzing with our heads. This book and the concept of going right is not an effort to motivate you like Mike Davis, it's an effort to rationalize the right approach. We don't need convincing that our goals are emotionally compelling. If, however, we understood the logically clear advantages to pursue our greatest goals, then following them would be easier.

That day, Davis's epic speech, reached us all. We all heard it, and we all believed it. More importantly, we all wanted it. The man in a Major League uniform was preaching to the perfect choir. This type of pep talk was specific to us. We all knew that we wanted to be professional baseball players. Life is full of pep talks telling us to follow our gut and chase our dreams. There is, however, a distinct shortage of people following through on those emotional pulls. It's not that people are failing in their pursuits, they're simply opting out of their dreams. And while pep talks are powerful, they aren't powerful enough. At some point, we decide that emotion doesn't pay the bills or give us stability. That our dreams were merely fairy tales made up of compelling monologues.

All those starry-eyed kids couldn't maintain the rigor and lofty ideals of that day. They all, to some extent, gave up. A disciplinary suspension for Ohger in high school was all it took for him to give up on baseball forever. Todd Smith played through high school and excelled at three sports, but never took it to the next level. Quinten Daniels continued to play baseball but discovered that his athleticism made football fun, too. The war drumming of a Mike Davis speech wasn't enough. At some point, going to an extra practice, committing to the extra work, or the pursuit wasn't worth the squeeze anymore. Despite the emotional appeal, they all quit.

Since I was the only one of that group that day who didn't quit, let's look at my process and the role of Mike's pep talk in it. I can say wholeheartedly that I was seriously impacted on that morning. Maybe I was affected the most. I was, after all, the guy who wrote the quote on my hat for more than a decade. Mike's quote, however, was nothing more than a helpful nudge. When I moved on to high school baseball team several years later, it wasn't the quote that helped me manage the fear of failure. In fact, seeing the quote inside the bill of my hat felt kitschy. I was physically overmatched as a freshman, but with a level of commitment and discipline as strong or stronger than my peers, I made the varsity team. I just couldn't run as fast, throw as hard, and swing as swiftly as my teammates. It wasn't the motivational speeches that propelled me. This is why going right is a framework for decision making that must be forged on much more solid ground than inspirational speeches. The road to your peak expression is far too long, far too arduous to propel your journey with peppy emotion.

→ → →

Every individual struggles to find their way and nearly every example of peak human expression isn't complete without a coach or a mentor.

As beautiful as pursuing my dreams playing baseball were, anyone who has pursued peak performance knows that there is always a fair share of struggle. When someone is as close to their craft as I was, it can be painful. Following my peak expression through baseball taught me a level of resilience. Naturally, I sought to hire a coach. Coaches, after all, aren't just for piano lessons and soccer. Coaches can do more than tell you where to position your feet in a batting stance. Even following the tenets of going right requires assistance. Coaching is a remarkable support structure to taking on the challenges of going right.

Enrolling a coach takes courage. The ego wants us to do everything ourselves. But the audacity of the task at hand was significant enough to ask for help.

My coach, Dr. Cara Miller, was one of my favorite professors in college. She taught the capstone course at the University of San Diego's leadership school. As an expert in adult development and organizational culture, Dr. Miller was a perfect choice. She is a professor, executive developmental coach, and leadership consultant, working for clients such as the Defense Department. She has also been Robert Kegan's teaching fellow for his course in adult development at Harvard.

Part of my intention in enrolling a coach was the total coaching experience, which includes teaching, challenge, and accountability. Dr. Miller taught me things about this process I couldn't learn on my own. Beyond essential foundational learning, deadlines, and assignments, there was ruthless accountability. I not only had to honor our friendship in the process, but I also insisted on a strict no discount policy. I needed to pay full price. It had to hurt, and it did, but, much like the scaffolding found in community support. Not only would my coach help take me to places I couldn't go on my own, but I was also accountable to a level that felt like no turning back. With one foot in the field and one foot in academia, Dr. Miller played a remarkable role in challenging the exposures that would make me the entrepreneur, athlete, writer, and coach that I am today.

Louie Simmons is an icon in strength and conditioning. The Ohio native is a stout figure, with tattoos covering a muscular body that has been pushed to the brink of peak performance. He's been broken and built back up time and time again. What's more impressive than the five decades of elite powerlifting performances is his ability to weather and recover from serious injury, including two broken backs. Louie is hard to follow as he talks extremely fast. He has an innate ability to remember lifts, records, and training percentages at a Mensa-like level.

Powerlifting and training are rife with controversy and disagreement, and Louie is right in the middle. The combination of a vast landscape of information and extreme passion are odd bedfellows. Take personal training, for example. A client reaches out for guidance and accountability. The trainer naturally falls into a role where it pays to be the expert. As a result, there's a stage set for exaggerated expertise and a downplaying of different approaches. Fitness is such a broad modality that, by nature, it includes countless movement practices, ideologies, styles, and preferences. It is often impossible to keep up with the names, practices, titles, certifications, and dogma. As I've mentioned, human nature doesn't do well with uncertainty.

Given this dynamic, there's a fertile environment for thought leaders, trainers, and coaches who feel the need for invention. There's a feeling that a trainer not only needs to be right, but they need to have secret keys to success. Secret keys can't, by definition, be old methods. This is why we get new practices such as P90X, Tae Bo, the Bowflex, and a thousand other fads.

Innovation is almost always of a greater utility than invention. It was Louie who said, "I didn't invent toilet paper, but I'm smart enough to use it." It's when you understand the foundation set before you then you may be able to contribute something new to further its evolution. Innovation can slingshot progress beyond current levels, in part, by piggybacking on foundational developments and learning from past failures, while invention would likely retrace the processes and failures of history in an effort to surpass it.

If you ever step foot into the world's strongest gym, you'll feel the culture in the air. The metal music and the sweat is one thing, but there is a thick atmosphere in Westside Barbell. This is the house that Louie Simmon's built. There is a professionalism that borders on savagery. Westside Barbell isn't just the world's strongest gym, it's arguably the most controversial, as well. While the countless world records held by the members of this private gym are primarily held in powerlifting, Louie would call himself a strength and conditioning coach, not a powerlifting coach. Like any leader in the fitness community, he is passionate about his methods. Few coaches, though, can support their methods as well as Louie when it comes to science, key principles, and a long history of world-class results.

At sixty-eight years old, Louie has deadlifted more than 700 pounds or more for more than forty years. The first athlete I met at the gym on my visit was Dave "Mr. 3000" Hoff. He holds the world record for combined—squat, press, and deadlift—at 3005 pounds. His one thousand pound bench press is a world record, as well. Hoff often wears a shirt that reads, "My bench is your squat." This, of course, is only a punchline if you're in a room full of one thousand pound squatters. At Westside, that's nearly everyone.

Louie's methods, known as the Westside conjugate method, are actually quite old. Louie uses "accommodating resistance," where the load being moved gets marginally increased as an athlete moves through the desired range of motion. The rationale for this is that the human body becomes more mechanically advantaged to move the load as it progresses through the movement. This is the reason, for example, that completing the bottom six inches of a full squat are most often more challenging than completing the last six inches at the top of the lift. Louie's methods often involve attaching giant rubber bands or hanging chains to the bar because the load is more progressively challenging. The skeleton of his program, however, is based on very old principles and methods and his tweaks and additions are efficient innovations. What's Louie's advice? Study the greatest in history, learn the principles, practice the techniques, and develop an expertise. Once you have a strong understanding of these methods, you can improve upon what's been done before you.

→ → →

Purpose and our connection to it are critical drivers in going right. Without purpose, we lack meaning in our lives. Purpose is so powerful that it always keeps us in pursuit of our goals.

Motivation, even in the most driven individuals, is a relatively unreliable resource for long, arduous pursuits. Discipline, however, is the ability to continue without the presence of motivation. It is the longer lasting, more reliable fuel source for going right. In that way, there may not be a better developer of discipline than having a strong sense of purpose in our doing. Life is full of struggles, often magnified when we take the going right approach. We feel like we are risking more by chasing these dreams. This is understandable. The gravity of the struggle puts a premium on purpose. When someone is on the long road to mastery and excellence, they're bound to confront failure, poverty, adaptive challenges, and unforeseen adversity. It's your connection to purpose that will transcend motivation and external praise or reward.

How do we foster discipline? We develop discipline when we have a strong sense of purpose. When we have a clear picture of the desired end goal and can claim a strong sense of purpose and fulfillment, we connect to the process that transcends motivation. A person with discipline will march forward regardless of the circumstances.

Pursuing a craft that gives us purpose is pursuing a craft with built-in discipline. Motivational speeches, pep talks, and other emotional spikes in desire can obviously help, but when they're gone there is discipline to propel us forward.

We've all thought and heard statements such as "I've always wanted to be a professional artist" or "I want to start a foundation to support women's rights," followed by some hemming and hawing. People claim they need to be realistic and find a paying job.

It's not about having a job or not. It's about finding purpose and self-actualization.

There are endless expressions of going right that extend beyond career choices. Every decision we make should be viewed through this lens. Think about how we, as humans, manage work when we're doing something we're semi-committed to. Is it easier or harder to work overtime at a job you'd rather not be working? How inclined are you to develop true mastery in an area of partial interest?

Not all expressions of going right are, or need to be, glamorous. The value that's created by those who follow this path is astronomical in much more relatable, even pedestrian, ways than chasing big league dreams, becoming a rock star, or a champion fighter. When people pursue their highest self in seemingly ordinary relationships, career expressions, and lifestyles, we can best understand the objective advantage of going right.

The best auto-mechanics, graphic designers, and burger servers are often on a journey to the fringes of discovering their best self. This is an expression we can all benefit from. After all, who would you rather trust, an auto mechanic who's checking a box or an auto mechanic who is living their passion?

I found a key example of going right when I needed to solve a simple problem. The strings on my baseball glove broke.

My father took me to an underwhelming shop in a Los Angeles strip mall called La Tijera Bootery. The store was a leather repair shop situated on a boulevard that diagonally cut across the Los Angeles grid like scissors, which is where the street got its Spanish namesake.

As a ten-year-old kid, I could barely see over the counter. My dad spoke with an older gentleman who examined my catcher's glove thoughtfully. I remember being confused because by all accounts this was a shoe repair shop. But then I noticed a small tack board covered with articles of baseball players from all over the country.

La Tijera Bootery was owned by Ben Brucker. Baseball players and coaches called him The Glove Doctor. If you cared about your baseball glove, you brought it here. Period.

Brucker wasn't just a leather guy who had the means to fix gloves. He took pride in baseball gloves in the way the Basquiat took pride in painting, and Dave Grohl takes pride in rock and roll. The career path of leatherworker might not ever be placed on a societal pedestal or appear in lights, but the contribution Brucker's work made to his life and the lives of others was nothing short of remarkable. The humble storefront of La Tijera Bootery would never do justice to his impact in the world of baseball.

Choices for fixing baseball gloves were, and continue to be, quite limited. You could try repairing your own glove. Or you could take your mitt to an apathetic shoe repair shop owner in hopes that someone with some leather knowledge would be able to do a satisfactory job. La Tijera did such good work that their impact made waves across the Los Angeles area and beyond. The shop turned out custom glove work not just for passionate local baseball players but also for iconic Hollywood films like "League of Their Own" and "Field of Dreams." Brucker's work can be found in Cooperstown, NY at the Baseball Hall of Fame.

The strip mall couldn't contain Brucker's influence. In the winter (baseball's offseason), he would work on as many as fifty gloves per week for amateur, collegiate, and professional players. In an article in the *Houston Astros* magazine, Brucker explained how he did business with a number of Major League players who need gloves quickly in the next city they're playing in. "An equipment manager or team manufacturer's rep picks up the gloves, and he brings or sends them here,' Brucker explained. "The reps give us an address, like Carmelo Martinez for Pittsburgh will be playing in St. Louis on such and such date. He'll tell us to get the glove there to the equipment manager a day ahead of time. We get it out so it'll be there on time."

Many of these players are making millions of dollars a year and are so exacting about the work Brucker does and the passion he has for leatherwork that it's worth sending their equipment from the dim shop on La Tijera Blvd.

"Ain't nobody does that kind of work," Brucker extolled in the magazine. "There are so many different things we do. Nobody does that kind of work."

Authentically continuing to pursue your peak expression comes with unmistakable advantages like being able to proudly declare that, in fact, "nobody [else] does that kind of work."

I'm not here to pile on with redundant ideas about pursuing your wildest dreams. I don't need to convince you that. But many of us deviate from the pursuit of these dreams largely because we deem them illogical. This is why we're going to skip the talk of how good you're going to feel doing your dream job, living in the best relationships, and expressing an idyllic lifestyle. I feel compelled to make an argument that seems silly but is necessary: better is better.

Yes, you heard me right. Better is better.

To start taking action toward going right, you need to begin to listen to yourself. All the thoughts you have about who you want to love, the life you want to live, and how you want to spend your time are your guides. You'll need to start building trust in the process, and believe that pursuing your dreams is more logical than avoiding them. Don't worry about not knowing the specifics of what to do next, the details of what your preferences are. The goal now is to use these desires that tap into your purpose and maximum fulfillment.

To not go after our dreams is a level of self-sacrifice that is emotionally unsatisfactory. Not only do we deserve more of ourselves, but our families, our communities, and the world deserve better. Proceeding towards going right and our best self puts us closer to an ideal outcome, even in failure. Because pursuing higher evolution and maximized value is a universally important pursuit. As fallible humans, we will always be a living breathing personification of imperfection. It's of much higher utility to experience failure heading in an authentic representation of our ideal selves than wasting it on natural human error in a job that diminishes you. Better is better.

→ → →

OK, I'll admit it, I'm a fan of Rocky. In Rocky IV, Stallone's monologue to his son highlights the emotional appeal perfectly. It's the same pep talk we discussed earlier.

Rocky squares up his son for some tough love. "Let me tell you something you already know," Rocky says, in a scratchy drawl. "The world ain't all sunshine and rainbows. It's a very mean and nasty place, and I don't care how tough you are it will beat you to your knees and keep you there permanently if you let it. You, me, or nobody is gonna hit as hard as life. But it ain't about how hard ya hit. It's about how hard you can get hit and keep moving forward. How much you can take and keep moving forward. That's how winning is done! Now if you know what you're worth then go out and get what you're worth. But ya gotta be willing to take the hits, and not pointing fingers saying you ain't where you wanna be because of him, or her, or anybody! Cowards do that and that ain't you! You're better than that!"

I don't bring this up in an effort fire you up. This is a message, after all, we've heard before. It's not about the successes, it's about the adversity. Embracing the struggle is part of the path.

But taking the going right approach isn't just a matter of enduring. We've already determined that regardless of the direction we take, we'll face adversity. Rocky knows this lesson because the *only* way is to take blows the face, get bloodied, and continue against all the odds. Going right isn't a mental exercise. It's a physical and emotional embodiment of progress. Naturally, there will be mental challenges, but they will always overcome that punch in the face.

Forget the gut check motivator from Rocky for a moment and to realize he speaks the ultimate truth only because he's weathering his perfect storm. He's able to endure the most significant storms with the largest lightning bolts because he's going right.

CHAPTER 11

SPILLED MILK

TAPPING THE BOTTOM of a metal milk pitcher on the counter, Nicely Abel is still able to hold a conversation with his customers, keep the drink orders in line, and produce masterful art. Nicely is making a latte and, I'm not exaggerating, there might not be another person on earth better at it than he is. While it may seem odd to discuss baristas in a book about the expression of true potential, let's not lose sight of the idea that there are classes of mastery in any undertaking. Nicely shatters the stereotype of a pseudo-barista pressing buttons. This is a master turned entrepreneur turned icon. His hands, lithely holding an espresso cup at a forty-five-degree angle are covered in tattoos. As are his arms and neck. Nicely's skill calls to mind a sign etched at the historic Renaissance-style hotel, the Waldorf-Astoria: "The Difficult Immediately, the Impossible will just take a few moments longer." What Nicely can do with coffee, believe it or not, seems impossible, and it only takes a few moments.

In the specialty coffee world of single estate coffees, boutique roasters, and professional baristas, Nicely is a household name. This semi-underground world of coffee excellence is filled with weekend throw-downs between dozens of local baristas and coffee aficionados. Even coffee has its own competition circuit. Nicely has been in the top tier of the World Latte Art Championships for years. He's won the title 'World Champion' three times.

Don't get it? You don't have to. Going right for you likely doesn't mean elite coffee making, but Nicely's discipline for his craft, and the pursuit of his purpose-driven potential is a case study in going right. Nicely got his start at Espresso Vivace in Seattle. Vivace is the anti-Starbucks. There are no sugary pump options there. They offer professional barista courses for $500 per day with a curriculum that includes extraction techniques and theory. People like Nicely go to work at Vivace to develop a craft.

Nicely deliberately chose and committed to a path. We know this because Nicely elected to work at a coffee shop built around learning and, most importantly, he didn't quit. He intended to spend his time learning from the best. And he accumulated a large body of deep work. Deliberate practice is our next level of going right.

On a recent sunny afternoon in July, Nicely was working behind the bar taking orders to keep the line from stretching too far, but he was also preparing for a shot at his fourth World Latte

Art Championship. There's an effortless freneticism to Nicely's routine. I stood respectfully trying to maintain my role as a customer as to not steal too much time from him. He's clearly working, and I'm feeling like a temporary input in a very well oiled machine that is the operation of his business. I remember unmistakable ease in his movement. While we're in a conversation, he's practicing. The custom seafoam green La Marzocco was made especially for the world champion's coffee shop that is just steps from the Pacific Ocean. I kept coming back to the intentionality of his effort. This practice isn't passive. This repetition is clearly contributing to his mastery and the specific lead-up to his competition. As he's knocking the bottom of the metal pitcher on the counter before pouring a beautiful rosetta, he explains to me how he's practicing for the upcoming competition. "In this event, I have three minutes, and I'll make two drinks," Nicely says. "The equipment I'll be working on there is faster, though, so I've been doing trial runs here with a stopwatch. I intentionally slow myself down, because I know if I can execute in this environment that I can have more time, and it will be easier on game day."

Nicely's approach to his craft is using the highest utility practice environment. Few baristas have a better mental representation of what winning latte art looks like. This is critical for Nicely's ability to improve with every repetition. While Nicely is already a world champion, he continues to utilize the clear stretch goal by perfecting his craft and testing his approach with slower equipment. He has a crystal-clear picture of his ideal pour, which allows him to get feedback instantly on each attempt. He has a level of intensity and focus, and an ability to make small adjustments from repetition to repetition.

Nicely has been engaging in strategies for years that put him in position to practice his craft in the richest of learning environments. This environment is called *deliberate practice*, a term coined by the psychologist Anders Ericsson, who we heard from earlier. Ericsson's work centers on research in the field of positive psychology and how humans achieve remarkable levels of mastery.

Ericsson posits that best practices for skill development must inherently be stressful to the system. Autopilot is the enemy because when we lack stress and focus on our repetitious practice, we begin to plateau. This is why our skills advance exponentially when we are initially learning any craft. Take, for example, the process of learning to drive a car. The stress and feedback of those earliest exposures— avoiding other cars and people in the road, and staying between those pesky dotted lines—enables skills to expand. The routine of driving later in life, without stress, doesn't allow the same learning.

Deliberate practice is the best environment to develop peak performance because its criteria continues to challenge the subject. What makes deliberate practice unique? According to Ericsson, the effort must be a clearly defined stretch goal. The desired outcome resides just beyond the comfort level of the subject. Next, the practice must offer immediate and informative feedback. This feedback is only possible if the person has a very accurate "mental representation" of the ideal outcome. People receive critical information that fuels their improvement in a very tightly wound feedback loop. This happens with each repetition when their immediate, informative feedback is contrasted against their ideal outcome. An Olympic figure skater needs to understand what a triple axel looks and feels like for the feedback of their practice effort to have context. In Nicely's case, he must have a very detailed understanding of a winning pour for his practice reps to inform him about the adjustments needed. Lastly, Ericsson says deliberate practice takes repetition.

I know what it's like to reach relative mastery in a craft. My craft was the sport of baseball. Accumulating the necessary work to achieve mastery is arduous in any pursuit, but much of the practice volume can become rote. I'd take millions of swings in my career, the majority of which came, at a young age, off a batting tee in my backyard. I'd hit hundreds of baseballs into a net each night.

Nicely is doing the same with a lot more wasted milk!

The process of becoming a top barista is relatively complex and generally expensive. Unlike hitting a ball into a net, each repetition for Nicely involves grinding coffee beans, tamping down the coffee, then extracting the coffee with a particular amount of pressure and water. The espresso needs to be mixed with milk steamed at an exact temperature for the right amount of time. And none of these processes is considered the actual latte art itself. Holding the cup a particular way is as much of a key as the pace in which one pours the milk into the espresso and how the strokes of the pour create the designs in the crema. That's just one repetition.

As with any practice, a huge percentage will be poorly executed. A person training as a barista could also do some practice reps at home, but what happens to all that unused coffee? Going through a gallon of milk, and a half pound of coffee and twenty lattes strewn across a kitchen counter, all for *practice*? Do you invite a dozen coffee-thirsty friends over? Do you have twenty mugs, or do you have to pour them out as you go? How do you realize your masterful potential in the art of coffee making?

At a successful shop, a barista can get as many as three hundred reps in a shift. Working a full-time schedule would require roughly seven years to create 10,000 hours of latte work. If you made three hundred drinks every day during the work week, you'd be steaming and pouring roughly 4,265 gallons of milk. Clearly, the commitment discussed earlier is critical to enduring the time required with the craft to form this body of work. In addition, the reps are too meticulous and too few and far between to make remarkable progress. Mastery is that much more elusive when reps are tough to come by.

In that way, Nicely admitted to being guilty of another habit we see in individuals accepting going right: spending extra time with the craft. Going above and beyond becomes normalized. Nicely will often finish his shift only to leave his apron on and make a few more drinks for additional practice. This is true going right behavior. This is being connected to purpose at work.

Because Nicely's repetitions are somewhat scarce, as a result, he needs to maximize the fruits of each labor. When there's a limit on how much practice is possible, you've got to make the most out of each practice rep. "Every drink that I am making is an opportunity to practice," Nicely explained to me quite matter of factly. I saw in his unspoken confidence the same confidence I recognize in masters in other crafts. What lies in the longer inhales between breaths during this explanation is the magnitude of his vast body of deep work. As a listener, you get a feeling that he's recalling lessons and insights from a much larger filing cabinet than most. The importance of each rep and the level of focus Nicely needs to evolve his craft isn't unique to him, or coffee making. Not all practice reps on the road to mastery are created equal. Some practice is unequivocally better than other practice. Those who are committed to going right find themselves not only more committed to their practice, they get more out of every minute of their practice.

According to Ericsson, being in a position to adopt deliberate practice matters more than we think. "In the long run," Ericsson writes in an acclaimed text titled *Peak: Secrets from the New Science of Expertise*, "it is the ones who practice more who prevail, not the ones who had some initial advantage in intelligence or some other talent."

→ → →

There is a false notion in the world that people can rise to the occasion. It has been proven—most notably in the quant work of baseball analytics—that there is no such thing as a clutch player in sports. John Welbourn, a ten year NFL veteran and founder of Power Athlete HQ, a training resource and educational platform, often says in his seminars, that "Time and time again we observe that we don't 'rise to the occasion.' Instead, we fall to the level of our training." The expectation that a football player with poor mechanics will miraculously find good mechanics against competition under peak stress is ridiculous. The same expectations are as absurd for a soldier to kick down a door and enter a compound and complete their mission if their training was solely shooting paper targets in a well lit, air-conditioned facility. We must do the work. There is no shortcut to peak human expression.

Cal Newport, a computer science professor at Georgetown, has written a number of books about work and study habits and self-improvement. In "Deep Work: Rules for Focused Success in a Distracted World," he carefully connects both deep practice and what he calls "deep work" as not just valuable, but increasingly rare. Deep work improves the quality of what we, as humans, are able to produce. Newport's defines deep work as "professional activities performed in a state of distraction-free concentration that push your cognitive capacities to their limit. These efforts create new value, improve your skill, and are hard to replicate."

When making decisions in life, these types of efforts are more natural and easier to sustain. Being tethered to purpose and a deep-rooted source is an understandable driver for the intensity of one's focus. Newport writes that "shallow work is non-cognitively demanding, logistical-style tasks, often performed while distracted. These efforts don't create remarkable, new value in the world and are easy to replicate." There's not a lot of value in work that is characteristically replaceable.

Newport makes the case that deep work and deliberate practice are quite valuable, and this is an age where they are becoming *increasingly* rare and *increasing in* value. In Newport's analysis, our emerging economy has three clear winners: highly-skilled workers, superstars, and owners. Those who will thrive in this emerging economy won't just be irreplaceable by intelligent machines, they will also work exceptionally well with them. Deep work is required practice to advance one's skill set from proficient to remarkable to create exceptional value. The interconnectedness of the world through "high-speed data networks and collaboration tools like e-mail and virtual meeting software have destroyed regionalism in many sectors of knowledge work," Newport argues. "It no longer makes sense, for example, to hire a full-time programmer, put aside office space, and pay benefits, when you can instead pay one of the world's best programmers, for just enough time to complete the job at hand."

Being good at something—a superstar—might get you far in some aspects of life (e.g., being good at baseball might get you a letterman's jacket), but it's worth nothing at the highest level. As the world becomes increasingly more interconnected, being good will become more meaningless than ever. That's the humbling news. Deep work, deliberate practice, and sure-fire best practices show up naturally because there's no such thing as making a living as the best shortstop in your city. Eventually, you'll need to be one of the best thirty shortstops on planet Earth to get that job. It pays, however, to have an obscure passion. Like Nicely.

Lastly, owners, those with uniquely large sums of capital, are largely able to succeed on the shoulders of deep work-type efforts. These sources of capital can fund creators of exponential wealth. Take Instagram for example, which was acquired for a billion dollars in only four hundred days with thirteen employees and no revenue. The creators of these explosive economic force multipliers are virtually married to the idea of deep practice. Breaking through the tipping point of being one of many to *the one* takes remarkable talent.

Taking deliberate practice to its logical conclusion and pushing through to a committed end takes grit. Angela Duckworth, a psychology professor at the University of Pennsylvania, the founder of Character Lab, an organization that studies character development, and the author of "Grit: The Power of Passion and Perseverance," is the foremost scholar on the subject of grit. She argues that the grittiness required to keep coming back to a craft is more important to one's success than talent. Duckworth's work has shown the importance of grit in a number of areas.

Her early work was in developing a better indicator of who would have success in West Point's grueling training program called Beast Barracks. The rigorous application process begins with a letter of recommendation from a member of "Congress, a senator, or the vice president of the United States." Only the highest SAT/ACT scores are considered. Grades must be impeccable, and athletics and leadership ability is viewed as a premium at West Point. Almost every student at West Point was a varsity athlete, and *most* were team captains. Even still, checking all these boxes is the equivalent to putting on your cleats for a soccer game. You're not even on the field yet. Despite the grueling application process and saturation of talent, West Point still wasn't able to predict who would make it through orientation. Talent and pedigree couldn't predict who would quit and who would stay. Interested at the prospect of getting to the bottom of this Duckworth produced the Grit Scale, a ten question survey to help predict success. The questions are not questions, but a series of declarative statements such as "New ideas and projects sometimes distract me from previous ones," which the taker must agree or disagree with on a five-point scale. The Grit Scale was not only unusually precise in determining who would survive orientation but indicated who would thrive in sales for a timeshare business, who would become Green Berets, and even which kids would place highest in the Scripps National Spelling Bee.

What's useful about Duckworth's work is that it illustrates that sheer talent is not an indicator of who will succeed. With a little grit, anyone can realize their dreams. It provides a roadmap for reaching those lofty goals. Duckworth was influenced by the academic paper, *The Mundanity of Excellence*, which looks at the training for high-level swimmers. The paper reveals that these athletes' remarkable accomplishments were surprisingly anticlimactic. Outstanding performances and achievements are a culmination of many unassuming efforts. The truth is that we are ultimately responsible for our success (or lack thereof) because we *are* as capable as anyone in fulfilling the potential of our dreams of going right.

With deliberate practice, showing up is not enough. There are no prizes for just doing the job. Clocking in and out each day doesn't make you Employee of the Month. I'd hate it if my friends took the same approach with our friendship. To take a going right approach, we must accumulate a *meaningful* body of work. The repetition required to actualize our best selves isn't a fly-by-night operation, either. You'll need to toil with your craft to be a good father, make an NHL team, become the best dog trainer within a thousand miles of your business, or whatever going right means to you. Not just *any* practice will do.

→ → →

A concept that originated with Anders Ericsson and was popularized by Malcolm Gladwell in his book "Outliers," is the 10,000 Hour Rule. This notion revolves around the idea that to achieve significant expertise in a skill a person must practice—deep practice—for a minimum of 10,000 hours. Gladwell noted that any and all masters first did the work to achieve their lofty status.

As a rule, none of the greats, regardless as to how naturally gifted they may or may not have been, accumulated their 10,000 hours before they had monumental success. According to Gladwell, the world's most iconic band, the Beatles, didn't explode into stardom as a unit until they accumulated well above the 10,000-hour requirement performing countless marathon sets. Bill Gates, too, wasn't just a lucky benefactor of technological timing or a born computer prodigy. He just so happened to get exposed to coding at an early age at a progressive high school in Seattle. This put him in position to log the necessary hours to become remarkable.

The 10,000 Hour Rule is not without controversy. A number of critics were outraged at the idea that we have more responsibility and control than is written in the stars. The idea that the only thing standing in our way is our own mental block sends people into fits. Nonetheless, numerous researchers and authors have moved the needle on the 10,000-hour rule since. Daniel Coyle, the author of "The Talent Code," points out that the rule isn't a green light for semi-interested dreamers to simply play ball for a while and suddenly become a pro. It is all in the type of practice and the mentality by which someone approaches those reps.

Not all practice is created equal.

Generally, all masters have logged their preparation time, while all who have logged their time are not necessarily masters. Passive, uninvolved practice doesn't quite pack the developmental punch that deliberate practice does. Practitioners of deliberate practice have a profound connection to their work which includes a feedback loop to make countless adjustments and refinements. Deliberate practice can hold us closer to our ideal trajectory.

→ → →

Take a moment and imagine the feeling of embracing going right. You've chosen that pursuit which you have great passion for. It's a decision that is outside of your current ability. The road to seeing this decision through includes, first and foremost, time with the craft. If it's a relationship, you'll need to water the seeds of love. If it's a career that both challenges you and gives you purpose, you'll need to bridge the gap between your current self and this future existence. There will be, in any endeavor, time under tension to cross the bridge to ideal expression. It's this process that deep work and deliberate practice are most critical.

In going right, the passion and connection to purpose supports deeper focus and greater volume and intensity of work. Those competing for excellence begin to apply best practices, receive a tight feedback loop, and make faster adjustments in strategy. Consider the environment of a job in which someone doesn't adhere to going right practices. Since there is no purpose in guiding the effort, the minimum effort is put forth.

The journalist Joshua Foer, author of "Moonwalking with Einstein," and the 2006 USA Memory Champion, used Ericsson's three elements of deliberate practice—clear stretch goal, informative feedback, and repetition—to perform remarkable feats of memorization, including memorizing a shuffled deck of cards in less than sixty seconds. "Deliberate practice," Foer says in his book "by its nature, must be hard." Deliberate practice pushes the stagnation of what is referred to as the "autonomous stage," where people are performing without thinking. The stage creates a plateau problem for people looking to get to the highest level. Foer notes that peak performing individuals "tend to follow the same general pattern of development. They develop strategies for consciously keeping out of the autonomous stage while they practice."

Tex McQuilkin, a strength coach and motivational speaker, often points out in his motivational talks that "95% of the world stays in this 'I want' Wasteland. I want this, but I can't. We need to get out of it." He's talking about the ease of desire and the difficulty of making it a reality. The problem highlights that achieving remarkable results requires remarkable process-oriented focus. Total immersion is a focus issue. Those in deliberate practice are rarely distracted. The focus must lead the desire for practice, addiction for another repetition, and an ability to overcome any dissatisfaction. Characteristic of deep practice is an advantageously short feedback loop, so those immersed in deep practice can get more information from mistakes and do so faster, which means improvements can be made exponentially quicker.

There is an acute disparity between our observed reality and our ideal vision of reality. It's this disparity which is the fuel that drives us in going right. This fuel is deeply rooted in purpose. The motivation to close the gap between reality and idealism comes from within, making it geographically closer to the body than social pressures and other extrinsic motivators.

As the practitioner accumulates time in deep practice, they begin to develop finer and finer awareness to their craft. As the skill of managing their practice becomes more experienced, there is more fuel to do more of the work. If we are hyper-aware during deep practice, then we understand our orientation with quality. Awareness is an understanding of context. From this, we get information about the direction and proximity to our idealistic pursuit.

By now, you likely understand the value of having a large body of deep work, but how do we create a large body of quality work required for mastery? Craft mastery comes at the end of the long road of practice. And not just any practice will do. Once you've developed commitment for a particular pursuit, you'll need to get to work. This is the crux of the challenge placed before us mere mortals. We want results, but focusing on the end results is not a helpful motivator. It's a focus on the process that is the catalyst for success.

Masters of their craft must log a massive volume of work. This work must be deeply focused and toiled with. If you're committed to the challenge of going right, you'll need to become process oriented. Time and time again the best form of practice looks like deep work and deliberate practice. Don't waste any time or effort being distracted by the finish line.

Since you'll be logging so many challenging hours of work to march your way towards your going right goal, you should feel supported by the previous stage of the journey. When the going gets tough in the process of developing a large body of deep work, you'll have your commitment to fall back on. It's the lack of commitment that is the graveyard of people not adhering to the going right approach. I'd quit too if I were 9,000 hours into something I didn't have a compelling, committed reason for pursuing.

As we pile on objective reasons for going right, we'll see that deep work fortifies us against the perils of adversity. Uncertainty is an opposing force we all are subject to. Resilience in the face of adversity will pay dividends during long, challenging pursuits. After all, isn't that why we prepare and engage in deep practice? We engage in the craft for the sake of the craft, but we also can conscientiously build a stronghold of preparation for whatever comes next. If the only true certainty is uncertainty, then the outcomes we're seeking are out of our control. However, those who are prepared, specifically with a large body of deep work, are more fit to thrive in the unknowable future.

CHAPTER 12

THE ONLY CERTAINTY
IS UNCERTAINTY

HUMANS DON'T LIKE the unknown. Albert Einstein was no different. According to Leonard Susskind, a professor of theoretical physics at Stanford University and the author of "The Black Hole War," Einstein loathed the mounting evidence of the unpredictability of the world. Susskind discusses our faulty understanding of determinism in his book. "The first thing that physicists had to free themselves of—the thing that Einstein held so dear—was the notion that the laws of nature are deterministic," Susskind explains. Even the most sophisticated models and elaborate laws of nature are no match for the uncertainty of our universe.

We're natural truth seekers. Humans ask why. As a result, we do what we can to assign meaning and explanations for the unknown. Uncertainty is a significant hindrance in simple decision making. Given a choice, it's easy to understand why someone might choose perceived certainty over the unknown. Not knowing is stressful. The fear of uncertainty is such a powerful influence that we question what our approach to a decision would be if we knew we couldn't fail at it. As a mental exercise to unchain our deterministically biased thinking, it opens up some interesting thinking.

What do we do to cope with the unknown? We avoid it. We suppress it. This behavior stems from a biological need to survive, seek safety, and increase the probability of reproduction. The problem with this pattern is that it often backfires. While it may seem like avoiding uncertainty minimizes risk, it often trades perceived safety for even greater risk.

This is a phenomenon that is rampant in the business world. College graduates choose their majors and career paths based on trends in the workplace and find themselves making disadvantageous choices as a result. On the surface, can you blame them? Going into an unpopular field is potentially risky. But what is the point of working in a hot job field that you don't love and cannot develop valuable mastery in? Putting in years of work without the benefit of deep work or purpose is just wasted time and effort. Being an unremarkable team member provides no value to you or to the organization. The lessons learned in the pursuit of our highest expression aren't available if we decide on the safe and compromised route. We don't learn humility, confidence, process, and how to manage wholehearted investment when we're not pursuing our true expression of self.

Take, for example, a person finding a life partner who says yes all the time. This may enable them not to be single and to avoid constant rejection, but their partner won't demand mutual development, won't hold them accountable, and might not be able to endure a lifetime together. If we're in the business of minimizing risk, this choice may work in the short term but is unlikely to last through the ups and downs of life and love. Yet, many people continue to take the easy route and not take a chance on happiness. This is a tragedy, and it's manifested in every other way we choose to spend our time. Our craving for some certainty can drive our decision making to the wrong choices.

The more we dig into risk management, projections and predictions, and contingencies for the future, the more we ought to realize that there is no way to map out a perfect path forward. Uncertainty *is* the only certainty. As the legendary heavyweight boxer Mike Tyson once said, "Everyone has a plan until they get punched in the face." In life, we're all getting punched in the face in one way or another. When we take a going right approach, we're better equipped to absorb that punch. We're better suited to weather the storm if we've made decisions that are aligned with purpose, self-actualization, and self-respect.

Who manages risk and uncertainty more than stock traders? They spend their time immersed in minimizing uncertainty. Nassim Taleb, a statistician, risk analyst, writer (and former trader), makes his money on uncertainty (he made nine figures betting against the housing market during the financial crisis before anyone else). In Taleb's book, "The Black Swan," he argues that no number of specific past observations can justify a general prediction of the future. As a rogue trader, Taleb makes money when others lose. He views an academic analysis of the market as a suckers game. No matter how often we're right about the future, massive unforeseen events continually wipe out national economies and markets rise and fall on mere whims.

Taleb illustrates uncertainty with the following example. One day a turkey is walking around on a farm when, around noon, a bell rings. A man walks out with a bucket of feed and throws some of it on the ground for the turkey to eat. Every day after that the turkey walks around the farm, hears the lunch bell, and eats. After a thousand days in a row, the turkey catches on. He understands the routine. In fact, the turkey becomes so sure of the routine that he's confident the next day will be like the thousand preceding days. What the turkey doesn't know is that day 1001 is the day before Thanksgiving, and the misguided bird will be plump enough for the meal. Rather than hearing the bell for food, the turkey gets plucked up and has his head promptly cleaved off. If he could speak, he would sound like every other market expert after a sudden drop of a company's share price. There's no way anyone could have seen this coming.

If uncertainty is pulling you away from your best self and the decisions it takes to evolve the highest extent, I've got news for you. You're lying to yourself. Taleb argues that despite all the powerful computers, academic study, and lengthy algorithms in the world, there is no magic solution to justify certainty. There is no magic number of observations of the past that can create accurate predictions of the future.

Not only are humans naturally fearful of uncertainty, but we are also susceptible to a fatal mistake, the narrative fallacy. The history of human evolution is rich with language and storytelling. If I asked someone to memorize a random sequence of fifty letters, it would be nearly impossible. However, if I arranged those letters into a sentence, the results would entirely different. Almost anyone could recall the letters in the correct order. The power of context and meaning within a narrative is incredible. Do you remember the fifty states song from elementary school? Those kinds of mnemonics are common because they provide the necessary context to facilitate memory.

Taleb's describes, in the "Black Swan," the fallacy as "our limited ability to look at sequences of facts without weaving an explanation into them, or, equivalently, forcing a logical link, an arrow of relationship upon them. Explanations bind facts together. They make them all the more easily remembered; they help them make more sense. Where this propensity can go wrong is when it increases our impression of understanding."

The moment there is an unexpected event, it's human nature to work backward to try to understand how and why it happened. Without these stories, so many events just wouldn't make sense. This tortures the human psyche. We look into history to find meaning and explanations that obviously couldn't be understood if they were revealed in real time. This is, Taleb says, being "fooled by randomness."

The key to understanding the prevalence of uncertainty and our tendency to try to make sense of the randomness is to accept the inevitable. When seeking a distant goal or desired outcome, uncertainty can be seen as adversity. It's how we deal with adversity that defines those who are taking on the going right approach and those who are not. If uncertainty is our only certainty, then we know life is full of bumps and hurdles. If we can handle them, then we have a shot at success.

→ → →

The inside of a casino can be a somber place. Most people at any given moment, after all, are losing. Pushing chips forward for another bet—whether you're on a winning or a losing streak—is rife with anxiety. Because we know the odds are not in our favor.

Imagine this scenario. You're at a blackjack table. You started the evening with $300 and quickly turned that into $3000. When it's good, it's good, right? Then you started losing. After a series of unexpected losses, you wish you could go rephrase that. When it's good, it's good, until it's not. The truth is, you didn't get up and leave when you had a fortress of chips in front of you, and that's why it's called gambling.

You're betting $50 a hand, which is more than you typically spend on a meal out. Your next bet calls for you to double down. All things being equal, doubling down is a mathematical no brainer when the cards line up. It's your best odds, even though every hand has you at a mathematical disadvantage. Real money is on the line, but you like the odds here. Two hours earlier, you doubled down twice in three hands and started your night up three grand.

As luck would have it, *this* double down comes in less fair weather than the last time. Your early run was a rush, and while it's easy in hindsight to say you should have walked away, here you are, back at square one. What injustice! You followed the playbook. You hit when you were supposed to and stayed when you should. Initially, it felt like a reward for following the statistical, emotionless guidebook. The dealer confirms you should hit, you do, and he subsequently takes your chips.

"Cut your losses. Get up," you mumble to yourself. The devil on your shoulder, though, says, with some authority, "You have to win it back before you cash out."

The injustice of bad luck is disorienting. Fearing another losing hand, you play against the script and hit when everyone, including the dealer, tells you not to. Such deviation from logic is irresponsible in gambling halls. But what does logic count for when you finally win a hand?

Winner! Winner! And, just like that, you're back. And what brought you back? Sheer, random luck. Despite this lucky hand, the truth of the matter is you're nursing a losing streak. An hour and a half ago, you had two whole stacks of $100 black chips to shuffle and fiddle with. Now there are only a few measly $25 greens. The problem with assessing the odds is that it's really only relevant when you're examining a large body of data. If you sat at the blackjack table for 24 hours, you might see the odds hue toward their prediction. But if you rely on a single bet or a single string of bets then making an accurate prediction is sheer folly. Uncertainty is the only certainty

Blackjack has a set of rules—"the book"—which is a royal we-like reference to the objective statistical realities of the scenarios in this game of cards. Blackjack, like life, has some elements within your control, like how much to bet and when to take a card, and others you cannot, like who gets what cards. While blackjack is a game of math and, as a result, more straightforward than the game of life, many of the principles are still the same. Since real money is on the line, which serves as real skin in the game, the uncertainty is more prevalent than ever. This is where we find you now. Emotionally, you're up and down. The book, however, doesn't change. Riding high or suffering through losses doesn't alter the mathematics of the odds. But these emotional elements can affect your behavior.

You'll never learn, will you? This is the plight of human nature. On a moment by moment basis, the realities of something as simple as blackjack can be distilled into basic odds and we can either give ourselves the best chance for success or not. Fate will take care of the rest. Hot streaks, risky play when the chips are low, confidence when the stacks of chips are high just reaffirms the odds. While we all share the desire for positive outcomes, humans are illogical. Sure, a robot would ultimately make the best blackjack player and logical decision makers, but where's the life in that?

This struggle between human emotion and logic extends well beyond the casino floor and into our everyday decision making. The same things that pull us away from your best chances for success at the blackjack table are the pitfalls that put us into the wrong relationships, lifestyle practices, and careers. When living with uncertainty, optimal decision making simply puts us in the best position for success. Fate will do with us what it may. Like the book, however, we might be able to make decisions that at least stack the odds in our favor.

→ → →

Albert O. Hirschman, a former German economist who died in 2012, was the author of several books on political economies and theories. Hirschman coined the term "Hiding Hand Principle," which refers to the idea that when an individual or group of individuals take on an intensive project, their own ignorance about the future struggles enables them to continue on, in the face of substantive obstacles, because they've made it too far to quit. After all, ignorance is bliss.

I can tell you fully that in every case in which I've made a significant decision to use going right principles in my own life, I did my best to imagine the significance of the struggle ahead. And every time I failed to see the hurdles that came. Luckily we can use the Hiding Hand Principle to our advantage.

At age seven, I couldn't have *fully* known the process of becoming a professional baseball player. I was, for most of my youth, confident about what would be required of me to attain such a goal. Not surprisingly, my calculations were way off. The Hiding Hand Principle showed itself in a number of ways, including injuries, failures on the field, and many others. I could imagine, at seven, that it would be a lifelong challenge and silly things like the feeling of striking out or losing would always hurt, but there is no context to the sense of failure when you've made fifteen years of sacrifices and commitments to succeed. The strikeouts when I was twenty-two hurt much more than they did when I was eight.

→ → →

Much in the same way that we've discussed how commitment provides the foundation for the pursuit of a large body of deep work, having accumulated a large body of deep work is a support structure for increased resilience to adversity. After all, who is more fit to battle adversity than those who are most prepared? Knowing that is half the battle, so it's also good to have a specific strategy to build up resilience to adversity in and of itself.

What is adversity? Adversity is the discomfort associated with undesirable outcomes. Failure, injustice, resistance, and a host of other external forces that impede progress. While it's completely understandable to try to avoid adversity, the way you think about these issues might be doing more harm than the adversity itself.

This is a crucial point. If you're on your way to becoming a high-performance individual, you'll need to think like a high-performance individual. High-performance people believe the elements in their lives fall into one of two categories:

1. that which you *can* control
2. that which you *cannot* control

If you're choosing to take the going right approach, it shouldn't be lost on you that you'll be confronted with a host of challenges along the way. By definition, if you're going right, you're choosing to explore outside of your level of preparation. This is in an of itself is a heavy dose of adversity. Adversity will likely come in the form of skepticism, unsupportive commentary, and even opposition from friends and family. Things aren't going to go as planned.

Sure, you'll be prepared (with your commitment and a large

body of deep work) for many of the trouble spots in going right, but the heart of what will help you navigate adversity will be your ability to put energy into that which you can control.

The reason this is so critical comes back to the utilitarian view we're talking about in this entire decision-making conversation. If our best selves are being cultivated by our own doing, we only have so much time and energy to do so. The strategies used to manage the uncontrollable elements coming your way are never better than the elements you *can* control. After all, the variables that you have a hand in controlling are the only ones that your effort can affect future outcomes with.

CHAPTER 13

THE HAT MAKER

WHEN THE GOING is good, it's hard to imagine anything but success and prosperity. As Robert Frost wrote, "Nothing gold can stay." Change is always looming.

On February 24th, 2009 President Obama addressed a joint session of Congress with humbling news. The United States was entering in the middle of dark economic times, the Great Recession. Most Americans had never experienced anything remotely like the economic crisis. Growth, prosperity, and abundance were the norm for the better part of the prior several decades. President Obama described a country blindsided with unexpected adversity. His words echoed the oak walls of the Congressional chambers and rebounded into the microphones that broadcast his message around the country. "It's the worry you wake up with and the source of sleepless nights," Obama said. "It's the job you thought you'd retire from but now have lost; the business you built your dreams upon that's now hanging by a thread; the college acceptance letter your child had to put back in the envelope." Obama was even more direct when he bluntly stated, "The impact of this recession is real, and it is everywhere."

As a young man, days away from my first spring training with the San Diego Padres, I suddenly found myself in an environment with adult responsibilities and adult requirements. I needed to support myself and plan for the future. I was glued to the television that day watching the President and looking for any kind of hopeful sign in Obama's speech. With my first job out of school, the economy mattered to me.

Between February 2008 and February 2010, more than 8.7 million jobs were lost and the gross domestic product fell by 5.1%, making it the worst period since the Great Depression. Many people lost their investments, and a huge number of businesses went under. This was adversity striking at people individually and the country as a whole. In true form, adversity didn't do a good job of letting us all know it was coming. Instead, President Obama was dishing out the hard truth. Batten down the hatches!

The period immediately following the recession was particularly troubling for retailers, especially in the fashion world. Combined with the continued shift toward online shopping, fashion retailers drew a particularly short end of the stick. Teen clothing giant Aeropostale was unable to recover from poor earnings reports in 2010 and later filed for bankruptcy. American Apparel marked one of the most iconic fall-from-grace business stories several years later. High-end retailers, which are often more immune to economic shifts, were affected as well. Fewer than thirty days after President Obama's address to Congress, Bain and Company's semi-annual "Luxury Good Worldwide Market" study reported a 20% decline in retail sale revenue.

This wasn't a good time to be in the fashion business. Some brands would survive where others closed their doors for good. But the dose of adversity that the Great Recession doled-out touched the country as a whole. It's easy to see the potential advantages of going right in the face of such adversity. If you were uncommitted, you were more likely to be killed off first. Up until 2008, there were many winners. People with money in the bank benefiting from perceived job security. For example, a tenured career at the ultra-luxury brand Chanel wasn't just a high profile job, it paid well, and proved (thus far) to be safe. Until December 29, 2008, when the brand cut 200 jobs. The Guardian claimed that the brand hadn't seen this type of adversity since Coco Chanel let her entire staff go at the start of World War II.

Three years before President Obama's historic address, a young third-generation hat maker from Mexico migrated across the US border for a chance to take his career to the next level. Alberto Hernandez is a self-proclaimed black sheep in a traditional Mexican family. The Hernandez family, namely his father and grandfather, are master hat makers.

I visited Alberto at his Venice Beach shop one day at the end of summer to learn more about his story. We sat in the back of his shop, which had a beautiful storefront of hats that outstretched the breadth of any imagination and tackled some hat-making business first. The back of the shop is where you'll find the real work to be done. It's idealistically less presentable than the front of the store, which is reserved for a high end shopping experience where prospective customers have their heads meticulously measured and can sift through an unlimited number of variables from straw or beaver felt, color, level, and style of distressing, shape, brim width, crown type, and the list goes on.

The back wall of the workspace, which feels more like an open garage has scrap felts, and styling accouterments scattered on the floor has signature shelving with hundreds of circular wooden cutouts stacked in columns that represented the exact outline of the customer's head whose last name is etched in sharpie on the side. The room was well lit from the summer sun making it easy to read the wooden cutouts on the shelf in the back. Catching a recognizable Gaga doesn't require much wonderment to know you're looking at a wooden Lady Gaga cutout, but you can't help but wonder if the block with "James" written below it is Lebron's or not.

"How big do you want the brim, bro?" Alberto asked me. After all, what's the point in talking to a master hat maker if you don't come away with a hat.

As I peppered Alberto with questions about his life, he was responding and hat building simultaneously. With a steamer, he began to manipulate the beaver felt with his hands, turning what looked like a circle animal hide into the most unique western hat I had ever seen. He periodically put it on my head between thought exchanges to check the fit. The details were his favorite parts of the design process. The Japanese wire that would decorate the crown. His signature rusty clothespin that would cut diagonally through the back. The clear flammable liquid he sprayed on it and then lit on fire. His calloused fingers spun and poked the hat, allowing the flames to damage it to his liking before putting it out.

"OK, bro, let's go," Alberto insisted as if the last nine minutes of magical hat making were eating into his lunchtime.

At lunch, over a couple of fried chicken sandwiches, he told me more about his humble beginnings. His childhood home was littered with sombreros and hat making supplies. Deciphering exactly where the line between hat making and everyday life began and ended was challenging. The craft *was* life in his home. In many cases, the substantial exposure to any craft at a young age usually results in a massive attraction or an aversion. Alberto, however, was enthralled. He identifies with the craft. Not only has Alberto always thought of himself as a hat maker, but it also gives him purpose. The roots of this purpose only grew deeper when, at a young age, he committed himself to master the craft. But he also had bigger and grander visions than the modest foothold his family had in the industry. Alberto wanted to shake things up.

In Alberto's hometown, San Francisco del Rincon, Mexico, there is a giant statue of a seated man hunched over crafting a hat out of two fists full of straw. In this section of Guanajuato, hat making is king. What Alberto and the entire town of San Francisco del Rincon couldn't have known in 2006 is that the young boy leaving for America would become one of the most renowned hat makers of his time. All in the midst of the greatest bout of economic adversity in a lifetime.

Alberto left his city and his family with a vision and a craft, but not much else. His family's business never evolved and eventually went bankrupt. Alone, Alberto crossed the border and landed in Maywood, California. Maywood is an industrial, low-income area in South Central Los Angeles which is notorious for drugs and gang violence, and not so much for hats. While Alberto was a formally trained hat maker, he harbored a vision of edgy self-expression made possible with something as simple as a hat. Alberto knows his hat history. He can regale a visitor with stories of how prevalent hats were in different eras of American society. How everyone wore a hat until President John F. Kennedy's admiration (his good hair tipped the scales). He can explain how different generations preferred different brim widths.

Imagine the audacity of a young boy from Mexico immigrating to a new country to make a fashion product very few people wear anymore. But Alberto didn't push the envelope on life simply to make a felt fedora. That'd be too predictable and boring for him. Alberto wanted to make hats his way. Not only would he need to get people wearing hats again but he'd need to convince them to wear hats of a unique style they'd never seen before. Alberto was bathing in adversity before he even got started.

Alberto first turned to the only connection he had, a man his father knew who ran a hat shop in Burbank. He hoped the man would give him a job, but instead all he got was the shocked face trying to communicate the audacity of such a suggestion. A job?!!?? The shop owner could barely keep the lights on, let alone to hire some kid with no social security card who barely spoke English. Alberto begged him to at least let him sweep the shop, take out the trash, and aid in loose ends. After humoring Alberto with a couple days of sweeping, he told Alberto that was all he had. In response, Alberto upped his ante and asked for a mentorship. He was shocked at the response he got.

"Cincuenta dolares para la semana," the shop owner told him.

Thinking he was hitting a stride with this hat maker, getting fifty dollars a week sounded like progress. "No, me pagas," the shop owner responded. Alberto suddenly realized he had misunderstood. He wouldn't be making money, he would be paying to learn. The shop owner simply said that while it may not make sense now, he'd understand one day. They struck a deal. Alberto would pay $50 a week for the mentorship until he could make a satisfactory hat.

Meanwhile, his life in Maywood was dangerous. To makes ends meet, Alberto turned to selling drugs. He was in a foreign country, was *paying* for a mentorship, and now was involved in a life of crime. This was not how he envisioned his future. He was afraid of immigration, afraid of the police, afraid of the local gangs. On the flip side, it provided a living. The internal struggle for Alberto was that it would have been a lot easier to give up the hat making all the way in Burbank. Streetlife was remarkably predictable and stable by comparison.

At his hat mentorship, Alberto learned how to make hats with materials he wasn't used to. There were some major technical and adaptive hurdles. Alberto learned the details of beaver felt. Before that, he had been primarily skilled in making straw hats. It was Alberto's first real hat—under his mentor's tutelage—that is a story out of a Hollywood movie, and which would change his life forever.

A regular customer placed an order at the shop and, the owner feeling Alberto had shown real promise, trusted him to make the hat. This was his first test and opportunity. In this spotlight moment, Alberto let his rebel tendencies get the better of him. This is what gives Alberto his style but it also what can get him into trouble. While making the hat, Alberto took the request to distress the brim to another level. He burned a hole in the brim. When he showed the finished product, the shop owner was disgusted and upset. He condescendingly congratulated Alberto on not only failing his first test but for signing up to pay for the replacement materials to properly fulfill the customer's order. Alberto apologized and agreed to pay for the materials, but under one condition. Alberto demanded that the shop owner let him display his hat for sale. If the hat sold, he could use those funds to pay him back for the damages.

Alberto recalls calling his father back home. He was feeling hopeless. Alberto's father would always be straight with him, and his words carried significant weight. Crying and scared, Alberto felt like he'd lost hope. He came to America and tried and had nothing to show for it. Even if he satisfied the needs of the shop owner, business wasn't good enough to get hired there and make a living. His father gave him the encouragement he needed to push forward. His dad didn't want him at home. There was nothing there for him there. He needed to stay and continue to work to make a life in Los Angeles.

A few weeks later, while Alberto was sweeping the shop, a customer wandered in. Business was painfully slow, so a rare customer was startling. Alberto avoided getting into a conversation as his English was still poor.

"This guy. He has cowboy boots on. Beautiful ones," Alberto explained to me in his heavily accented English. "And, jeans with a lot of holes and rips here and all the way down in front. Bro, he has no shirt. No shirt. And long hair, kind of shaggy, you know? Big sunglasses, and a fur coat. It's a fur coat, like crazy, that goes from his shoulders down all the way to the floor. And, he comes in and turns right to my hat."

Caught between the butterflies because this oddball man was interested in his hat, and his fear for not being able to converse correctly, Alberto was frozen and stupefied.

"Hey, do you have a mirror?" the customer asked.

Pumping his wrist with a held up hand as if instructing him to wait, Alberto nervously dropped the broom and turned the corner to get the shop owner. Alberto knew immediately, from the shop owner's reaction to the customer, that something was up.

The shop owner walked him to a mirror and then scampered back to Alberto. "Do you know who that *is*?" he asked.

"No.."

"That's Steven Tyler!"

"..."

"From Aerosmith!"

"..."

Alberto didn't know at the time that this was one of America's most iconic rock stars. Tyler bought Alberto's hat and told both of them how much he loved it.

The next words out of the shopkeeper's mouth were music to Alberto's ears. "Can you make ten more of those?"

And that was only the beginning. Alberto would soon head up production at a new hat shop in Venice Beach, and he'd make hats for countless other celebrities from Madonna to Pharrell to Lebron James. Today he charges several thousand dollars a hat and has a waiting list more than hundreds of names long. Do you need a calculator?

Not only do people all over wear Alberto's creations, but the trend in hat wearing is making a slow and steady comeback. Just like Alberto dreamed of. I often wear a hat made by Alberto and receive regular compliments on it. Alberto's pursuit is too compelling to ignore. Alberto's newest label, Meshika Hats, is standing on its own in the hat making scene and the reverberations into the world are beautifully disruptive.

All rational logic pointed away from pursuing niche hat making as a viable life choice in a foreign country amidst the most significant financial downturn in recent history. What Alberto earned by pursuing his passion was a connection to purpose and a craft that provides undeniable value regardless of economic or fashion trends. When you're excellent, you earn job security, among other intangibles. That includes all the work he'd done to obtain mastery, as well as a resilience that could (and did) withstand anything thrown at him.

→ → →

Resilience is a powerful force in humans. Academia continues to examine what resilience is, who has it, and how to foster it (for individuals as well as organizations and communities). Resilience takes on two general forms. The first is the ability and efficiency in recovering from adversity. The second is the ability to sustain momentum amidst adversity. This second type—a kind of batten down the hatches approach—is fueled by a connection to purpose. When we're debating whether to stay the course, it helps to have a reason why. Purpose keeps our efforts on the rails, especially when there is virtually no reason to assume a successful ending. Or, to put it more succinctly, without a sense of purpose, there is no purpose to sustain.

This was a lesson I learned the hard way in baseball, where a nearly endless list of actions are out of your direct control. It can be demoralizing to hit a 95 mph fastball 400 feet only to have an outfielder make a diving catch. An out, after all, is a failure. The mind-numbing injustices in baseball can leave a right-handed hitter wondering if he should try to try batting left-handed instead. The magic on the baseball field is the same magic required of those who will be most resilient to adversity. It's when we detach ourselves from the results, which are out of our control, and commit to the process, which is in our control, that our chances for peak performance are greatest.

We all have our reasons when we deviate from our idealistic goals. I'm human, and I make excuses, like anyone else, when I eat unhealthily, slack on training, and cut corners at work. Adversity shows itself in many ways. Fatigue, financial stress, and unforeseen forces weigh on me, but the prevailing feeling is that I have more footing to justify showing up to something if I see purpose in it. It's in my expression in going right that I'm least likely to make excuses and deviate from my purpose-driven path.

Going right develops more immunity to adversity. It's the experience we gain through life, and dealing with all that's thrown at us, that helps to give us resilience. A successful practice in the early days of any adverse endeavor benefits significantly from a strong connection to purpose.

Legendary basketball coach Pat Riley perfectly describes the intersection of success and adversity in his book "The Winner Within" by saying that any team or organization will be struck by "thunderbolts" of adversity. "It comes from out of the blue," Riley writes. "Thunderbolts are unexpected catastrophes beyond anyone's control. Successful teams accept that not everything will always go as planned and that even adversity brings some lessons well worth knowing. But in any adversity, the seed of equivalent benefit bumps you up, or should."

Going right, with a deeper connection to purpose, a more resilient approach to life, and more commitment makes you tougher. Thunderbolts of adversity wreak less havoc on the people prepared for life's uncertainties. Fleeing from your passion (to, say, cashing checks as an insurance agent) doesn't shield you from the facts of life. Nor does it protect you from disease, heartache, or financial uncertainty. I know who I'd rather have on my team when bullets start flying, and that's the person who'd rather die than be somewhere else. Going right makes you thunderbolt ready.

I'm probably overly optimistic, but I find real pleasure in adversity. I have a nearly morbid attraction to it. When I encounter it, I'm convinced I'm headed in the right direction. Without it, I feel I am deviating from my best self.

Several years back, on an overcast June day, I found myself driving around Los Angeles trying to hawk a Tag Heuer watch (a college graduation gift from my ex-girlfriend's mother). I was desperately trying to build DEUCE Gym, but we were at least two months away from our first day of business and being run through the meat grinder of municipal politics. I was taking a break from helping my co-founder, Danny Lesslie, from gutting the bathroom to try to sell my watch to cover our looming rent dues. We did all the manual labor ourselves. The days were long, and the surplus of work challenged us in every way.

Our business went on to become a success, but at that moment it seemed like it would never come together. Every time I left a jewelry store that offered me a couple hundred bucks, I envisioned Coach Riley's face. I loved the struggle, but this felt like a never-ending thunderstorm. With a four-month delay on our opening because of permit delays, we were wildly over-budget. Being told you cannot proceed with your operation for reasons out of your control is a type of lightning bolt that is particularly painful. But our resilience—not the watch—is what brought us through.

The depth of our passion made each permit rejection feel like a deep cut into our bellies. As if it were a point of pride, we'd walk away from agonizing delay after agonizing delay steadfast to reach our goal. Without any cash flow, we were hamstrung, and the struggle was compounded by our lack of control over the pace and the outcome of the hurdles we had to jump through. But we were committed.

With our backs against the wall and no one willing to buy my fancy watch, I dug deep. The previous month I liquidated all of my modest assets to supplement a personal loan that would fuel this project. Forget about being a hard hitter, as Rocky would put it, I was getting hit hard. Fortuitously, I remembered some old saving bonds my neighbor had given me as a child "for college." At the bank, I discovered buried treasure.

"Are you sure this is right?" I asked. "Yes," she replied, "we doubled checked. You have $7250."

We were back in business! Well, not *in* business per se, we'd have to wait for proper government signatures for that. But we would be able to survive the journey.

And yet, this small victory was way too good to be true. The bank had made a clerical error, and the $7250 was a mere $725. Cue the lightning. Roll the thunder.

These little struggles seem insurmountable at the moment. Looking back, they are simple bumps in the road to a successful finish line.

→ → →

Throughout this book, we've looked at the underlying implications of going right and its influential effect on adult development. The approach laid out in this book is a catalyst for expanding our consciousness, but it's important to dig into *why*. As I've mentioned, we must transcend and include past stages to evolve into something more complex. The action that facilitates moving from one stage to the next is key because if evolution is what we're after then knowing how to evolve is vital information.

Researchers often describe adverse life events as catalysts for development. Otto Scharmer, a professor at MIT, a leading academic in the evolution of consciousness, and the author of the change management method and book "Theory U," is working to help people and organizations break out of unproductive patterns and find new areas of growth through decision making. Scharmer writes about how he was transcending his current stage of consciousness when he pulled up to the scene of his house burning to the ground as a child. This fire was a massive thunderbolt of adversity in his life. For Scharmer is was a kind of out-of-body experience where he realized that he was not his past or his possessions. Anything that challenges your assumptions breaks your developmental frame. This frame shattering experience is cataclysmic for growth to a new, more complex frame. What emerged from that lightning bolt for Scharmer was a newly developed state of consciousness.

If adversity is conducive for transitional growth experiences, then it stands to reason that putting ourselves in adverse situations can broaden our horizons. We often use the fear of these conditions as a reason to avoid them. This is what happens when people concede dreams and other idealistic life expressions. If development and transcending our current self is an underlying goal and life responsibility, then pursuits ripe with challenges ought to be the preference.

Consider the value of timing. Timing is something that happens to you. The decision to buy a house on the gang-ridden Abbot Kinney Boulevard in Venice Beach in 1981 can be viewed as bad-timing (and folly). But owning that home thirty years later—now one of the most desirable addresses in Los Angeles—the timing seems prescient. They can then defend their position with confirming information.

Timeliness, on the other hand, adds control. It's self-authoring. Timeliness could have said 1981 was an opportunity. Those who embrace timeliness seek disconfirming information (the current housing market has upside), see mutuality (this house in 1981 is both good and bad news), and is self-authoring (time is happening to me, but I have a say in what emerges).

Are you subject to timing like a helpless observer, or are you interested in what emerges from the timeliness in your life? In this chapter, we've determined that those people going right are more fit for these lightning bolts of adversity. The academic study of adult development corroborates this. Going right advances the mind's development, and equips us with frames better fit to handle bouts with adversity.

CHAPTER 14

IN THE ZONE

IN THE SUMMER of 2015, skateboarder Vanessa Torres was only three weeks sober. Torres, a professional skateboarder, was competing in the X Games, broadcast live on ESPN, after a multi-year hiatus from substance abuse. In 2003 she was a gold medalist, the first woman to ever win in skateboarding. In 2004, she took silver.

Torres, who is slight at 5'2", skates with the passion and determination of someone who can handle the bumps of scrapes of street boarding. She was a spunky kid from Anaheim, CA, who began skating at thirteen by trespassing into abandoned pools, empty lots, and empty buildings. She was persistent—grinding on rails, perfecting kick-flips and nose grinds, jumping down increasingly larger concrete steps—and gained, over the years, continually increased skill development.

It took seventeen years for her to get to her first X Games. But it wasn't just skill. It was an ability to stretch her capacity. She continued to pursue uncomfortable and increasingly difficult environments. In the case of skating on hard concrete, that can include a number of broken bones, plenty of blood, and a whole lot of frustration.

There are some sports, like golf, that seem unrecognizable at the highest level to how it looks at every other level. Skateboarding is the same way. The street style of most skateboarders is unrecognizable to the pomp and circumstance of the ESPN's X Games. In Torres' illegal escapades in Southern California, there were never more than a few friends with her. Sometimes they might have a camera. Though it was hard to pack real gear and lights in time when the fear of the cops is around every corner.

The event Torres was competing in, called "Street," involves a series of tricks in a street skating environment. There are handrails and ramps and stairs. But no cops. Technically speaking, her large body of deep work on a skateboard had never been more voluminous, but the challenge of competing at the highest level in skating was coming after more than a decade out of the sport.

Now proud of her sobriety, going right set the stage for a moment that would transcend everything that had already transpired. The commitment it takes to earn a spot at the top of the skating game *and* endure a ten-year hiatus with substance abuse only shows up when we're choosing our peak expression.

"As soon as I dropped in, all the nerves had dissipated," Torres told me recently. "I landed my first trick, which is always the deal breaker if miscalculated as it tends to throw off the entire run as you're trying to recover, and instantly tapped into this headspace where it was just me on the course doing what I love."

I met Vanessa after she shattered her knee filming 'Don't Quit Your Day Job,' a film about female skaters. As a trainer, my job was to get her strong enough to return to competition. That challenge, as well as her substance abuse, is something that we know folks who are going right are most fit to endure. And she did.

What would sustain an effort like Vanessa's? Commitment to her craft, for one. A large body of deep work, as well. Vanessa was skating in Street finals, sober, with ten seconds left to spare in her run. "Whether or not on a competitive platform, it was the best I had felt and skated in years. I executed my run flawlessly and," Torres recounted to me. "Even had ten seconds to spare and decided to push myself to attempt a trick harder than I'd ever tried in practice." READ: peak preparation and peak challenge.

"That's when the flow happened."

Torres was "positioned perfectly on the course" en route to a chest-high ledge. What would be less than ten seconds in total would be the accumulation of an entire life's work into the unknown. She would need to lean heavily on her first 10,000 hours to even have the jumping power to reach a ledge that tall. The never before executed trick would call on monumental skill transfer from masterful reps nearly twenty years in the making. The mental fortitude to operate in this critical moment among the distractions and external pressures of the crowd, the cameras, and the clock running out are all make-or-break skills that are earned over a lifetime of work. This stretch of ten seconds is only made possible with a lifetime of choices going right over and over again.

"I just went for it and nailed it, perfectly," Torres continued. What was just a few minutes felt like an eternity as her brain took in more information than normal with superhuman processing power to do the impossible. This slide on a high ledge punctuated a life long pursuit into Vanessa's peak expression and marked her return to the world's stage. As she landed the trick and rolled into an eruption from the crowd, time would expire, and the judges would award the legend yet another place on the podium at the premiere skating event in the world.

This brings us to the next amenity. Going right affords us the opportunity for the peak human experience of flow, which is when our best performances come with meditative ease and pure joy. The idea of Self washes away into the living breathing, highest utility nirvana known to man. Flow can be found at the intersection of peak preparation and peak challenge. Vanessa knows this intersection well.

→ → →

It's clear by now that going right is hard work. And this achievement-oriented view of life is opportunistic. It would be fair to ask "What if I just want to be happy?" You wouldn't be alone in asking that.

The Greek philosopher Aristotle said, "The human good turns out to be the soul's activity that expresses virtue." Happiness is inexorably tied to virtue. Happiness isn't something that just happens to us, it's something we work at to achieve. When we embody virtuous behavior, we experience deep satisfaction and fulfillment. Becoming a happy person is not different than being a great baseball player—it takes practice. Happiness, like going right, is a process.

Viktor Frankl, the Austrian neurologist from chapter 5, touches on the same idea when he said, at the talk in Toronto, "don't aim at success—the more you aim at it and make it a target, the more you are going to miss it. For success, like happiness, cannot be pursued; it must ensue... as the unintended side-effect of one's personal deification to a source greater than oneself." The purest pursuit of happiness is characteristically built on top of both positive and negative experiences.

This brings us to flow. Flow is an elusive concept and one that can be difficult for many people to grasp. Quite simply, flow is being in the zone. It is a mental state of being where a person feels fully immersed and focused on a particular activity or process. Being in the flow is to be in an uninhibited expression of human will. Time is altered, thinking fades away, and the body becomes a direct extension of the mind. Flow was recognized and the term coined by Mihaly Csikszentmihalyi, a Hungarian-American psychologist. Csikszentmihalyi was the head of the psychology department at the University of Chicago. Though the concept, in some variations, has existed for years, his introduction of it into the psychological lexicon has had brought implications across a range of scientific studies.

Flow can show up anywhere in any activity. It can be in a backyard game of H-O-R-S-E where you can do no wrong on the court; it can be in a conversation with an unrestricted thought exchange. True peak human performance, or the tip of the flow pyramid, takes work, though. The greatest expressions of flow come to us at the intersection of peak challenge and peak preparation. Flow is always a stretch ahead. When we're committed and resilient, with an opportunity to stretch, we can transcend and include our previous self into something greater than we were before. The exemplary performance in game 5 of the 1997 NBA Finals by Michael Jordan—flu-ridden and on an IV during half-time—was one of sports' greatest expressions of a flow state.

The mechanics of flow are meticulously connected to the experience of happiness. Flow requires Zen-like participation in the moment. We recognize flow only in reflection of it. Stepping out of the moment to notice and name the experience of flow is guaranteed to interrupt the experience. Flow is resistant to negativity. Dave Grohl touched on the magic of flow when he said, "When you're on stage headlining the Reading Festival you're not wondering how the court case is going to settle, you're revelling in the moment of one of the greatest nights of your life." Flow is happiness. If, then, we can distill the purpose of human life to something such as being happy, pursuing flow ought to be our purpose.

Flow is not only an inherently happy experience, but it is also remarkably high in utility. Isn't this what we've been searching for all along? At the end of the day, we write better stories, throw more touchdowns, experience more profound affection, and cook better meals when in flow. The happiness quotient in flow is greater than all pseudo-pursuits that serve as a distraction from the going right.

How do we get to a flow state? The strategy and order of development of flow follows the route we've explored in this book for going right. Commitment, deep work, and resilience move the needle towards a flow state. If you have greater skill development met with greater and greater stretch challenges, you begin to create more powerful flow states. But flow, like our previous steps, is not easy. It takes work.

Flow is permanently connected to context. The deepest expression of happiness for a toddler may come from a shiny red ball. But those same toys rarely fulfill the happiness needs of an adult. Watching your child walk across a stage to receive a diploma, however, does fulfill those adult needs. That moment in life came after years of struggle—tantrums and talking back and years of adolescent behavior—which in turn creates a richer experience. If we could bottle that moment, we would. Csikszentmihalyi reaffirms the in-the-trenches requirements of flow when he writes, in his book "Flow: The Psychology of Optimal Experience," "It is not enough to *know* how to do it; one must *do* it, consistently, in the same way as athletes or musicians who must keep practicing what they know in theory."

The captivating nature of flow is not only in the richness of the experiences, it is, in and of itself, self-fulfilling. Experiencing flow in a relationship can mean stronger, deeper, more passionate love; flow in a career creates more value for all stakeholders; flow in lifestyle pursuits provides better performances, faster learning, and more enjoyable practices, as well as more satisfaction and mean-making fulfillment.

Steven Kotler, a leading expert on human performance and flow, and the author "The Rise of Superman: Decoding the Science of Ultimate Human Performance," claims that flow has the utilitarian benefits of the highest possible performances, and is inherently fulfilling. Kotler, who also is the co-founder of the Flow Genome Project, an organization attempting to map the genome of the flow process, writes that "During a peak experience the individual experiences an expansion of self, a sense of unity, and meaningfulness in life. The experience lingers in one's consciousness and gives a sense of purpose, integration, self-determination, and empathy."

Kotler argues that the pursuit and experience of flow is a metaphor of the meaning for life. Humans are hardwired for exploratory behavior and are looking for new territory as much as new experiences to provide fulfillment and meaning. Flow is affected by dopamine, norepinephrine, and endorphins, anandamide, and serotonin, the combination of chemicals which produces a level of pleasure that is unmatched. It is just a matter of tapping all the right elements to create that perfect cocktail.

When the challenge and the preparation are low, we experience apathy. If we take any challenge and put our skill level at zero and increase the challenge slightly, we experience worry. If that challenge is high, we experience anxiety. Put me in a boxing ring (something I have no skills in) with a nine-year-old, and I'd be apathetic to the task. Exchange the nine-year-old with a high school boxer, and I'd be worried. Me in the ring with a professional? Consider the anxiety attack real.

Flow, at the intersection of peak preparation and peak challenge, is where the world's best performers live. The world's best surfers seek the biggest and best waves, and they want to be pinned against the toughest competition around. The science behind flow has shown us that risk, like the presence of challenge, is *required* to experience flow. It's the process of exposing ourselves to greater and greater challenges that move the needle on what it even means to be challenged.

Laird Hamilton once told me he feels envy for beginning surfers because they can feel flow on the smallest of waves. Laird, on the other hand, needs cataclysmic, death-defying waves to ignite that response. But Laird's advantage—surfing a hydrofoil at fifty miles per hour on a fifty-foot wave—is that he is experiencing a deeper, more profound flow. We must work for peak expression of ourselves. As the stakes of the challenge increase so does the need for preparation.

$$\rightarrow \; \rightarrow \; \rightarrow$$

While the pinnacle of any pursuit is a worthy goal being at the beginning of any endeavor isn't inherently bad. Elementary flow experiences are as important as peak ones but most important is to embrace progression. Flow is rooted in a natural progression.

The natural building blocks of the flow experience mirrors that of going right. It would be impossible for a young Dave Grohl to have the skill development to rock a stadium full of screaming fans without toiling with his craft. And I wouldn't have the skill or opportunity to step into the batter's box in the NCAA Regional Tournament if I hadn't practiced and prepared all my life. A progression of relevant skill levels and challenges is required to compound the effect to make these examples possible.

Since no master profession skips the amateur stage, everyone must accept the humble beginnings of any pursuit. Built into these decisions to take the going right path are early days of confusion, curiosity, and informal participation that may or may not develop into something more formal. It's a fools game to window shop for peak flow experiences at the end of the spectrum. Everyone must start small. We earn our happiness, just like we earn the right to surf big waves, rock sold-out stadiums, and hit big home runs.

Embracing amateurism, mentorship, and humble beginnings ought to be fun. Csikszentmihalyi highlights exemplars for their simple pursuits of flow in his book. These people are searching for fulfillment, not a profession. Csikszentmihalyi looks at people such as Albert A. Michelson, America's first Nobel prize winner in science. Michelson had fuel for a life's work studying the velocity of light, which he described as "so much fun." The more fun the process is, the more resilient we will be to adversity, the more we'll accumulate a large body of deep work, and the more we'll be committed to it all.

Flow and the happiness it creates is a process fueled by our control over ourselves in our environment. Csikszentmihalyi reiterates this critical point when he writes "the importance of personally taking control of the direction of learning from the very first steps cannot be stressed enough. If a person feels coerced to read a certain book, to follow a given course because that is supposed to be the way to do it, learning will go against the grain. But if the decision is to take the same route because of an inner feeling of rightness, the learning will be relatively effortless and enjoyable."

→ → →

Regardless of what conscious stage mind you have, flow still represents peak human performance. The elements of flow do not align with one's developmental stage. We will all experience clarity of goals and immediate feedback, a high level of concentration on a limited field, a balance between skill and challenge, feeling control, effortlessness, an altered perception of time, the merging of action and consciousness, and immediate return on invested energy.

Flow can't be bottled. The moment we note and recognize that we're in flow, it goes away. In many ways, the relationship between flow and consciousness is immediate. Flow removes the space between us and our consciousness. It's impossible to worry, have fear, or be distracted in flow. It makes a beeline for the heart of our own conscious. It captures our complete awareness.

When we reflect upon how flow shows up in our lives, past flow experiences, and future flow pursuits, our stages of consciousness come into play. Young children in the early first and second stages of consciousness, it can be argued, experience flow more often than any adults do. That's what play is. A series of semi-structured goals and challenges in the form of a child's game can elicit flow for hours on end. As we move through stages of consciousness and into adulthood, we tend to play less, of course. Yet, flow, too, can evolve. Remember the criteria for flow includes a relationship between skill and challenge. To chase flow means to chase more skills and increasingly challenging scenarios to institute them in.

If the activities that support skill development, increased challenges, and flow states are not socially supported, we may begin to disassociate with the environments that are flow opportunities.

If we start to conform to the socialized understandings of what people our own age, gender, and social circles do, we're no longer guided by internal or intrinsic motivations and passions. We've then become reactive to society. If society thinks it's weird to play the piano as an adult, you'll likely give it up and the flow states it brought you.

Right at about the time that the socialized mind is most chronologically common in people in early adulthood, I was still playing baseball. While I was playing at a high level at the NCAA Division I and professional level, I was playing a child's game. Regardless of what people think that experience is like, the friction is there. It's in these upstream battles that flow can be a savior.

Flow is not just an individualized experience. Dave Grohl gets to impart his flow experience on millions of fans. We're naturally able to recognize and benefit from the utility of someone else's flow state. It's possible that these states, when shared, can be contagious. Moving fast and loud from note to note with timing is challenging, especially in front of thousands of viewers hanging on your every movement. With Grohl's concentration peaked, his maximal effort is magically effort*less*. Time slows down. Then, there are thousands of individual flow experiences made possible in the crowd. After all, if you've had a nirvana poster on your wall for ten years or your first kiss came with a Foo Fighters track playing in the background, seeing and hearing those notes live makes the hair on your neck stand up. You scream louder and all the sudden you too, are walking into that same time altering fully present space. This is flow.

Flow is a summit that is fully and completely self-fulfilling. It's autotelic. In other words, it's worth pursuing for its own sake, not just for the individual but for every interlocking circle of communities. When going right we are afforded the more general, invaluable developmental learning alongside the more specific pragmatic learning. In the same way that Tait learned fighting, Nicely learned latte art, Alberto learned hat making, and I learned how to hit a baseball, we also learned so much more. Discipline, deliberate practice, resilience, and flow states are compelling skills regardless of application.

CHAPTER 15

NO SINGLE PATH

WHEN CARL PAOLI was a young kid, he used to fantasize about standing up on an Olympic podium, looking over a sea of adoring fans, and bending down to accept his gold medal. From an early age, Paoli was a gymnastics prodigy. He was born in the United States to Swedish parents and grew up in Spain. For fifteen years, Carl's commitment to his Olympic vision was nurtured by unbreakable compliance to the rigorous training days in the gym that always began, and ended, with the athletes lined up, standing tall, feet together.

Growing up, Paoli was a fearful kid with extraordinarily low self-esteem. Gymnastics was, for Paoli, a way to build up confidence. As a kid, he was on a mission. His peak expression was gymnastics. Across his young career, Paoli would become one of the premiere gymnasts in Spain, including winning a national gold medal in vault. His success led him to a premium camp with the entire national team to earn a spot on the Olympic team. He had done the work, sought to manage that which was in his control and ignore that which wasn't, and was now on the cusp of realizing his dream.

It wasn't until he was at the camp that he realized that he was an underdog. "I stood there," Paoli told me one day in my kitchen on a bright and warm spring day. "And I thought, I'm going to give this every ounce of me. If they say no, it will have to be to my very best effort." Paoli dove into every drill and training evolution that day with everything he had. He pulled no punches and attacked every ring, vault, and floor routine with a lion-hearted effort. Looking back, Paoli noted that after it was over, his lungs banging against his chest, he finished with a clear conscious. "That was everything I had," he said.

We were sitting at my kitchen table eating eggs, bacon, and drinking Americanos, staring out over a few swaying trees in the morning breeze. Paoli, an old friend, is a regular at my house and the conversation flowed naturally.

Paoli's gymnastics camp ended in the same way it began, with each member standing shoulder to shoulder. Carl's hands were bleeding. At some point in the day, he doesn't know when, he tore them, but he soldiered on. I had given it his all. "I'll never forget standing there, blood dripping from my hands to the floor," he said. "When we broke from our line, I left two small puddles of blood." He said nothing. His coach said nothing. The fifteen years of practice, falls, tight landings, teachings from his coaches, and the ultimate pursuit culminated with two small pools of blood on the gymnastics mat. His best wasn't good enough.

Today, Paoli goes by Coach Carl, and he's now a movement specialist and coach and the author of the book "Free+style Connection," which details an open source language of movement that provides a framework for full freedom of expression from action sports and fitness to basic locomotion and getting off the toilet. Shaken by the rigorous rules and conservative style of gymnastics, Paoli's message encourages freedom and unregulated movement expression. He has transcended gymnastics and has made impacts in the extreme sports community, break-dancing, and CrossFit as a thought leader and communicator.

Paoli is the antithesis of the dogmatic approach of gymnastics training. He helped develop a growing global brand called STR/KE MOVEMENT that manufactures and sells shoes and active sportswear for creative movement. While Paoli's youth was forged around the ideas of rule following, today his life today cuts against the grain that formed him. Free+style is a language with the ability to connect, discuss, and express movement across all disciplines. He encourages his readers and followers to take Free+style and mold it, break it, share it, and make it their own. As Paoli writes in the first line of his book, "Don't let other people's thinking limit yours."

After gymnastics Paoli was un-moored in determining the right life path. He worked in a marine biology lab for a stint but ultimately returned to movement. Paoli took a comfortable and familiar role, teaching at a local gymnastics school in San Francisco. Not feeling comfortable with how he learned movement—there's one way, and one way only—and falling into that same trap in his new job, he began, to evolve the message. No longer would his athletes line up, standing tall, feet together, and be forced to do one monotonous tumbling session at a time. Paoli's big breakthrough and his initial move toward going right began when he transcended the dogma of his gymnastics career.

Paoli's life today surely includes his gymnastics background. He never would be where he is without it. You've got to know the rules to break them. Paoli's commitment to the craft as an adolescent evolved from curiosity as a fearful kid lacking confidence to a young man who learned a level of commitment to gymnastics that would carry him through tough losses and a constant fight for supremacy among his peers. He carved out a growing skill set and continually challenged it.

→ → →

Most skills in high-level gymnastics appear, on the surface, far too specific to create benefits outside the gym. However, if you look closer, it's not so simple. Where to put your hand on the pommel horse during rotations may not translate directly to the boardroom, in writing, or public speaking, yet these are the areas that Paoli now thrives. Through his years of practice and training, Paoli knows commitment, dedication, attention to detail, work ethic, and the abilities to navigate the elements of being on a team. Over fifteen years of challenging himself, he is well acquainted and honest with himself. These are the skills that pay, literally and figuratively, outside of gymnastics.

Paoli now travels the world teaching seminars on his Free+style Connection for movement. At the beginning of each seminar, he talks about skill transfer. He describes a perspective where all basic human movement, even something as basic as a push-up, can have the ability to transcend its immediate purpose and be applied to innumerable applications in life. How you do one thing can be how you do another thing. This is skill transfer. When going right, the commitment, deep focus, and resilience one learns become immediately transferable to any other endeavor.

Recently, Paoli was invited back to consult with the Spanish gymnastics team about how to better understand movement. More than a decade after Carl said goodbye to gymnastics and his coaches, without a word, hands bleeding, he returned. Paoli's insights *include* his past, rooted in the very teachings from the Spanish gymnastics system. But that isn't why he was called back. He was called back for the part that makes him unique. The part he's *transcended* to become.

→ → →

If life does not have a single path, then it's clear that to live a full life skill transfer is king. Skill transfer is the general ability to take the essential practice of one thing and effectively using it to contribute to the practice of something else. It means that any time spent in one endeavor is not wasted. If a person is pursuing the seminary for a decade and then shifts gears, they could use their lessons learned and skills acquired in the seminary to be a more complex, high-value teacher, for example. I'm no longer a professional athlete, but I spend the bulk of my time coaching human movement and speaking about leadership. And I apply all of my approaches from baseball to what I do every day.

Going right provides for skills that are transferable to any endeavor, as well as access to an entire realm of skills relevant to high-level human expression. There are transferable skills across the board in any undertaking that maximizes our potential. Natural to these top-level pursuits are intangible values such as purpose, drive, commitment to the mission, failure management, clear communication, discipline, feedback awareness, and a standard of excellence. Not only do high-level pursuits encompass these qualities, but they also prepare people to use them as they evolve.

Excellence in any field has a way of revealing best practices. It's these practices—the habits, characteristics, and qualities—that are at the heart of the idea of skill transfer. Skill transfer explains why a former US Navy SEAL platoon commander can go on to lead a division of a Fortune 500 company. That person understands more than running a business meeting; they understand clear communication, leadership, management, pressure, and a standard of excellence. This example can work for anyone going right, whether they're moving to the boardroom or the art room. There's always a learning curve to get up to speed, but if a person has learned the fortitude of going right, they will be ready to adjust to anything.

Skill transfer gives people exploring their true expression

a chance to test and fail. The insurance of skill transfer gives people license to pursue their best self without fear of missing out. Choosing to do the thing that is at the heart of our deepest desires and purpose is the best learning environment to study for our next journey. An honest walk down the path of going right can feature countless career changes, relationship evolutions, and lifestyle practices.

It's not only the lessons we learn in taking the going right approach which are transferable, but it's also the experiences we go through as well. In an interview with Joe Rogan, host of the Joe Rogan Experience podcast, Steven Kotler, gets to the heart of skill transfer when talking about flow. "One of the things about flow is, the more flow you have," Kotler told Rogan, "the more flow you have and flow will cross domains. If you end up with a lot of flow while surfing or fighting or whatever, it will start bleeding into your other work because it's just a focusing skill, right? It's training the brain to focus more and in a particular way. You can train it up, so the more flow you have the more flow you have. There's huge boosts in performance that you'll start getting in surfing and it will start bleeding into your writing, and suddenly everything in my life started clicking and then my writing started producing a lot of flow."

→ → →

It's generally true that nobody wants to spend their heart and soul on an effort that becomes a dead end. It's important to understand that going right isn't an accuracy test. It's human nature to weigh the outcomes of choices based on the perceived ability to get the desired result. When dealing with seemingly large decisions that have a lasting impact, like where to work, who to marry, and what lifestyle habit to subscribe to, I empathize with concerns about our own accuracy in predicting what we're truly destined for.

The trouble with the idea of accuracy is in the premise that we're destined for something specific. When it comes to chasing our dreams, we can be fooled into thinking we have a particular life path. Are we actually meant to be a marketing executive or a school teacher? Nobody is destined to be anything that specific. Not a rock star, a strength trainer, or a development coach. The details of the decisions we make and the process we take is a more telling arbiter of our true self-expression. I'd be missing the point by saying my place in the universe was destined and defined by a modern game when men run around an enclosed park chasing a leather ball. Seeing beyond what we do enables us to move freely about our career, relationships, and lifestyle looking for the challenging choices that can evolve our expression of self.

Here's yet another prank on humanity. Despite the markers in life we imagine measure success and quality—a particular career for example—there's no telling that the quality of the work we produce is our true expression. Take Pat Tillman, former NFL star, for example. Tilman gave up his fame and fortune playing football to become an Army Ranger, where he tragically died. It's the reason why successful people aren't happy and why seemingly great marriages end in divorce. Only you know if you're pursuing your peak expression. Only you will know if you're going right.

→ → →

In September of 2003 I was a senior at Saint Monica Catholic High School in southern California. While many of my classmates had college applications on their minds, I was already wrapping up the process of committing to a school where I would play baseball. I knew what the next four years held long before my classmates did.

In a candid conversation one day after Spanish class, I mentioned to two friends the schools I was flirting with. Their reaction was surprisingly unsupportive. "Don't be stupid," one classmate exclaimed. "This is about baseball isn't it?" "What if you burnout? It happens all the time. Baseball isn't forever, you know?"

What I couldn't have articulated then but what I know now is that burnout is a symptom of a prolonged effort fueled by external motivations. Think of all the child prodigy pianists who give up after a decade or two working at the craft. What forces continued to put them on that bench with their hands on those keys? Overbearing parents? Peer pressure? The perception of others? This isn't a renewable energy source. When life gets arduous, extrinsic motivation just doesn't burn bright enough. Herbert Freudenberger, a German-born American psychologist, has spent his career studying burnout and stress. Robert Kegan, in his book "In Over Our Heads," writes about Freudenberger and quotes him on burnout, which is "almost always an indication that the person's goals have been externally imposed. Somehow he embarked on his present course because it was expected of him. He was never the authentic source of his choices, and consequently, they afford little real satisfaction."

The intrinsic motivation which propelled me during my baseball career afforded me the motivation to accumulate the work in deep practice, and it safeguarded me from any burnout. Once we're aware that a perceived outcome isn't our ideal reality, we lose the motivation to go that extra mile. What once was the fuel of our hard-charging, committed, deep practicing, resilient flow states, now is just hard work without the purpose.

People are ever-growing and adapting, and we evolve. We have few clear missions in life. Our only job is to evolve. We are meant to change course from one pursuit to another in our lives. Life, and going right, is never a straight line.

The very nature of going right is the process of evolving. Since we can't possibly know everything that we don't know, we will very likely gain unexpected perspectives in our pursuit of this goal.

Life is long, and it's impossible for expressions of going right to be the same when we're young vs. when we're more mature. The evolutionary path is not a single fork in the road, it is a network of deviations with opportunities to multiple directions almost moment to moment. We have free will to opt in and out of even the most stereotypically committed circumstances imaginable. Marriages have divorce, and life even has suicide. We are faced with trillions of these decisions in a lifetime.

Understanding the level of control, we really have in our lives often takes a certain mindset.

→ → →

Much of my decision making to take the going right approach in my life has left me with many valuable skills. My journeys through baseball and entrepreneurship have brought me the very progression that I've outlined in this book from understanding true commitment with purpose and the ability to work deeply to earning a resilience to life's inevitable adversities and even understanding deep flow states. When considering the hyper-relevance of all these characteristics, it's not hard imagining the value of these skills in any new context.

Deep practice paid dividends in the form of results on the baseball field in the same way it pays dividends everywhere else in life. After all, a shorter learning curve is advantageous in any pursuit. Commitment, then, isn't enough. Commitment can keep you coming back for years, but, like any pursuit in life, you can't just trade time for skill. You don't get promoted to the next level of mastery by turning in a time card. Deep work expedites mastery. What made me excel faster at baseball than my peers wasn't just the sheer volume of my body of work with the craft, but also the intensity of focus that made one minute of my practice more valuable than one minute of many of my teammate's practice.

As life would have it, uncertainty will rear its ugly head. On a long road to peak expression, everyone faces adversity. With flow, the complexity of craft mastery becomes effortless. When you've experienced it, you follow it. The only way to progress peak human performance, or a flow state, is to advance skill and engage in challenges that meet (and stretch) this skill.

When people choose to take on the going right approach, there is no finish line. We can and should return to new challenges and new evolutions. It is not only about moving from one career to another. It is about embodying the purpose and skill set and decision-making tools of going right in everything we do for the rest of our lives. The challenges, by definition, must be challenging. Commitment, deep work, resilience, and flow help in any pursuit. But you will need to transcend and include all of the painfully enjoyable stages of going right genuinely and authentically each time you step out in that direction.

This has been quite a journey through the unique advantages of an authentic pursuit of peak expression and ultimately what we're calling the going right decision making. From understanding discipline as a means to work more deeply and using craft mastery to become more resilient against external forces culminates in what we know as flow or peak human expression. This is a perfect environment for the development of highly transferable skills and conscious development. As we'll see, the value of these attributes and the urgency surrounding our need to evolve consciously is not just individually significant. Collectively, we can benefit, too.